PRAISE FOR THE ARTWORK OF JOHN L. KOEHLER

"*Works of Art* by John Koehler is a refreshing journey of an artist pushing the boundaries of his own imagination. When you have an artistic ability as expansive as John's, there are galaxies awaiting your exploration. John's work shows incredible courage to push past his perfectly polished sense of illustration and design in search of new visual horizons. The style of his work is already one of a kind in the marketplace, yet John carries forward, driven by an obsessive passion for the artistic muse. It takes a true artist to lead the way into such beautiful and imaginative realms of the unknown."

—**Peter Bragino**, Artist, Musician, Writer, Teacher

"John and I met at an advertising agency. Our offices were beside each other. We became fast friends because, like his art, he spoke from his heart. He nicknamed me Pepper and I called him Salt.

"To this day, it brings a smile to my face. I describe him as gifted, loving, zany, theatrical, unforgettable, rated G fun for the whole family.

"About his art, I could go on and on about the roller-coaster ride I took while reviewing his art. Surrealism, realism, portraits, and exploring the renaissance, knowing so much more is to come.

"Infinite possibilities of expression are at the fingertips of a person with heart, soul, dedication, laughter, and a color palette with ideas always being explored. I love the work. I love the person."

—**Terry Wilson**, Artist and Creative Director

"I **LOVE** John's work. It makes me smile. His art draws you in with the unusual subject matter, design, and layers of color. His work is playful and interesting with a little bit of quirkiness, just like John!"

—**Johanna Tydings,** Owner of 21st Street Art Gallery

"In the tradition of Van Gogh, John Koehler, in this wonderful narrative and collection of self-portraits, is not just looking at himself, he is reflecting himself in the world around him. Koehler is showing us a positive trait the average American has lost. Who doesn't want to meet the person trying to see themselves in you? How much better would we be to show that kind of compassion for one another?"

—**Nathan M. Richardson**, Poet, Author, Frederick Douglass Historian

"I consider it quite the privilege to count gifted artist John Koehler as my friend. Throughout the years, I've watched with respect and often amazement as he would bring to life beautiful pieces of art using different mediums. Each piece is a bespoke expression of John's unique and creative gifting. His art brings joy to me, and each year I look forward to seeing where he goes next with his art."

—**Scott Rigell**, Member of Congress (2011-2016)

"John's artwork is an extension of his personality—it's bold, it's vibrant, it's unapologetically fun, humorous, and always has a story to tell. I greatly admire both his concept and image exploration, as well as his dynamic use of color. The result is a joyful experience, especially for this admirer. And we can all use more joy. Keep creating, John, and keep us smiling!"

—**Kim Nelson,** Creative Director & Designer, Red Chalk Studios

"John's fertile imagination is only matched by his virtuosic illustrative techniques."

—**Glen McClure**, Photographer, www.glenmcclure.com

"I've followed and loved John's work for years, and particularly his most recent digital artwork. His bold and often humorous take on a variety of subjects is the perfect showcase for this ever-expanding age of digital painting, and it's not surprising to see John at the forefront. His evocative portraits beautifully add life to his subjects while showcasing the talent he's honed for many years with sweet enthusiasm."

—Mark Edward Atkinson, Photographer

"As an art educator, one of the particular areas that I focus on when viewing a body of work is the growth associated with the artist. I already know John is talented, but to see how he continues to push himself and his creative process is inspiring."

—Mr. Christopher J. Buhner, Education Specialist, Visual Arts Coordinator, Department of Teaching & Learning, Virginia Beach City Public Schools

"John Koehler's work is a kaleidoscope of color and fantasy. He draws a Warhol-like world of pop culture and patterned playfulness. This book peaks behind the curtain of Koehler's creative process, a rare gift into the mind of an artist."

—Andy Chaleff, author of *The Wounded Healer*

"I first met John in 1994, soon after I started working at the Family Channel cable network as director of creative services. John had just started his studio and was doing freelance work. I hired John as an illustrator and photo retoucher many times. He produced many incredible pieces for me. I would describe John (Johann, as I usually call him; he calls me señor) as extremely talented, as an art director, illustrator and fine artist. I admire his dedication and pursuit of perfection. His Procreate pieces are wild, whimsical, and interesting—I love them!"

—José Barcita, President & Creative Director, Barcita & Barcita, Inc.

"John Koehler has been a friend and creative partner of mine for—Lord!—twenty-five years now. We were paired for some corporate healthcare projects not long after he moved back to Virginia Beach and established his studio. As strictly a 'words girl,' the art direction side of the house has always been very mysterious to me. This book, then, was both illuminating and great fun—wonderful to see what John's been up to in recent years, and how his process has evolved (especially as he integrates the 'tools, toys, and techniques' of the digital age). His enthusiasm and energy are palpable. The writing is simple, clear, and cogent, and yet burns brightly with John's personality, giving it just the right touches of humor, approachability, honesty—and the perfect balance of genuine humility and (what I consider to be) 'earned cockiness.' The work depicted is provocative and lovely, and the text is an insightful telling of his artistic journey."

—Maggie Brydges, Writer & Editor, Word Brydges, Inc.

"My father has always been an early adopter of technology, especially technology for creating graphic artwork. I still remember the story of the hand-letterer from one of his early advertisement jobs who was angry he had convinced the company to purchase Macintosh computers because it would 'put her out of work.' But that's the thing about my dad—even though he was trained as a traditional media illustrator, he never shied away from using technology to create art. He saw it as the future, and so he evolved and expanded his technique. *Works of Art* is a collection of his newest digital photo illustrations created with the Procreate app on an iPad Pro, which he mastered years ago, admittedly leaving me in the dust. Each series shows different subjects and styles, some playfully neon-bright and others inspired by Renaissance paintings. I couldn't be prouder to see him share this collection with the world."

—Danielle Koehler, Author and Illustrator of *The Other Forest*

"I have been with John on this amazing journey of his since the 1970s where we met at VCU in undergraduate school. His growth and development over the years has been amazing to watch. I owe him so much for showing me how to master photoshop in its early stages and putting up with my lack of knowledge on the digital side of things which is a testament to his strength as a caring, sharing teacher along the path to success. His appreciation of my own airbrush and paintbrush skills that developed over the years took my own art to the next level, and my adoration of his work hopefully played some small part in taking his work to the next level as well.

I still have some of his early work, including a fantastic zinc plate etching of a court jester that clearly exemplified the direction he was headed—hilarious, outgoing, fun, full of life, and full of what DaVinci called 'Sfumato'. He embraced the unknown fearlessly and energetically with the enthusiasm only John could possess and has arrived as a fine artist in his own right. This is clearly evident in his piece, "Adoration Of The Mermaid", which transcends reality into a surrealistic world of aquatic imagery that sends us into sensory overload."

—Ed Obermeyer, Fine Art Painter and
Surf Photographer

"John Koehler tells a fascinating story of his evolution into a boldly creative digital artist. His explanations of technique lead into a series of extraordinary themes that he explores. A treat for any creator or art lover!"

—Bill Campbell, Artist

"John Koehler's art has been an inspiration for me since the 'Ducks & Dunes' days of the 1970s. At that time, John's masterful pen-and-ink drawings celebrated everything we loved about growing up in what was then rural Virginia Beach, Virginia. Over the years, it's been a pleasure and a privilege to watch John's artwork grow and evolve. His digital renderings continue to inspire and push the boundaries of artistic expression. Couple that with the wonderful work John has always done in support of his community and you have the double-edged sword of a life well lived."

—John Lee Reed, Creative Director & Artist,
Johnreedesign Inc., www.johnreedesign.com

2018-2022

WORKS OF ART

JOHN KÖEHLER

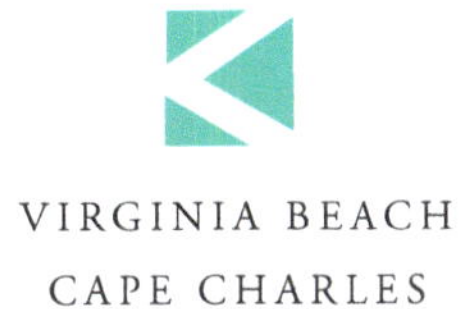

VIRGINIA BEACH
CAPE CHARLES

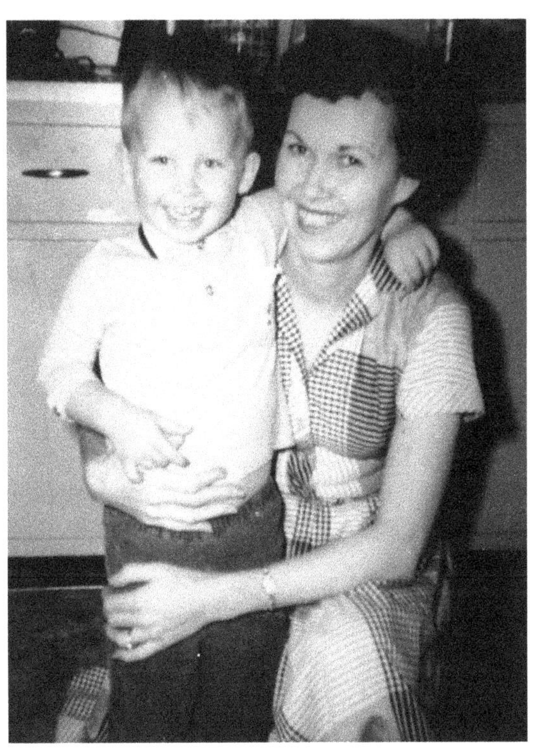

Artist John Koehler, age 4, shown with his first art patron,
his mother Mary Etta Koehler.

IN THE BEGINNING

I was not born with an art brush or pencil in my hand, much less a digital pen. Of course, in 1958, digital pens had not yet been invented, yet I seemed to have some early ability to see things and put them down on paper. This natural talent did not seem strange to me. It just was normal.

To me, it was the same as being able to throw a rock a long distance, with accuracy, or to pop a wheely on the move, or hit a baseball a mile. It was no big deal. Talent among boys was respected and expected.

My mother noticed my artistic talent right away, of course, and her interest in my own development was a bedrock element in my growth over the years. Knowing that someone not only loved me but loved the art I created was wonderful.

My elementary school teachers noticed my talent and put me to work creating bulletin boards, an early form of advertising, which eventually I got into later in life. I thought it was fun, and it got me out of some classwork. For the most part, I was a good student, As and Bs, but maybe a bit lazy.

I never took elective art classes until my senior year of high school. I was in Art 1, stuck with low talent, lunkheaded freshmen. Mrs. Woodhouse (may she ever be blessed) had us draw shapes and shade them. Duh, so easy, anybody could do it, right? Apparently not, and after two projects, she had seen enough, and moved me back behind the screens with the Art 4 and 5 students. True artists. "You're going to work on projects back here," she said.

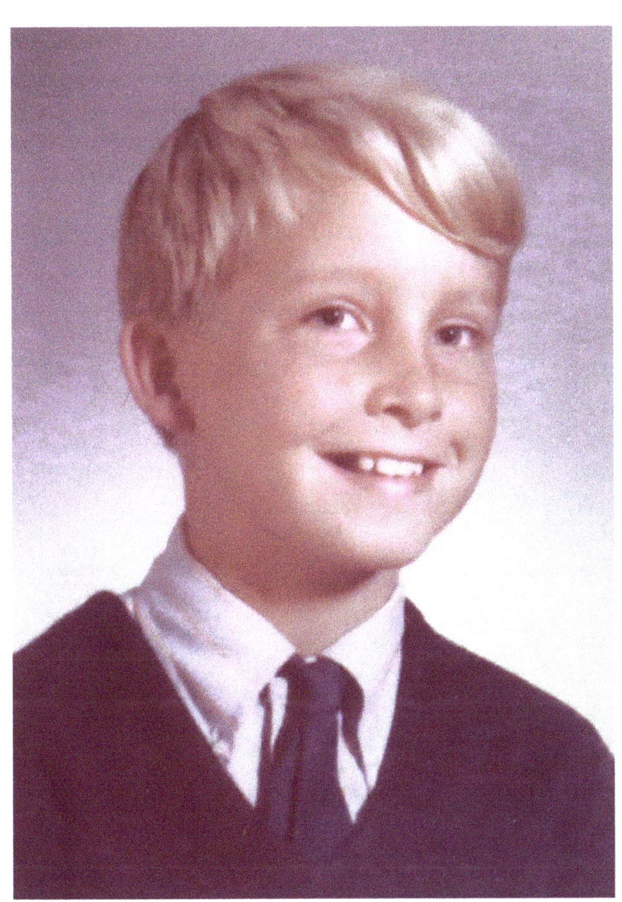

The artist in elementary school.

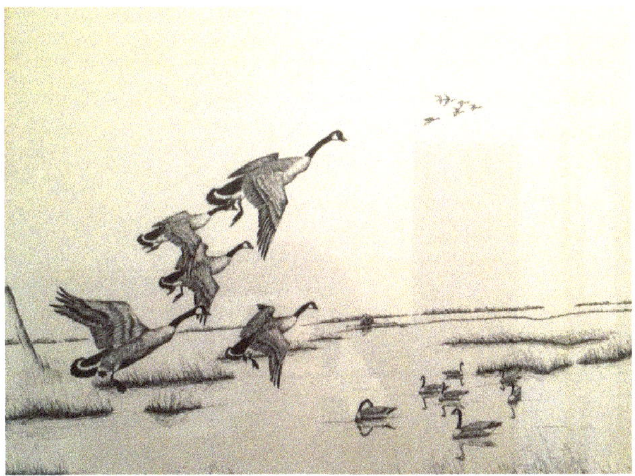

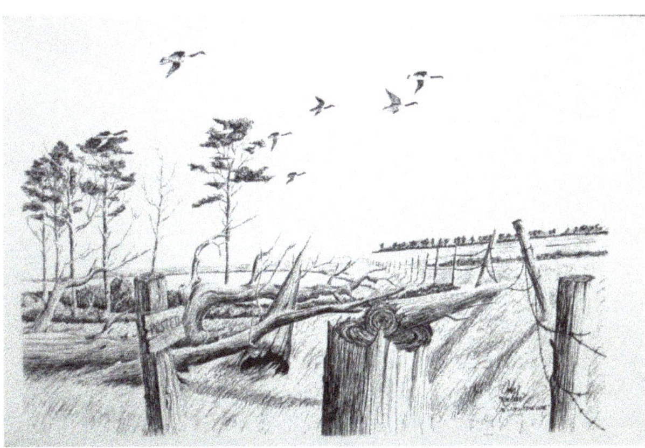

Pen-and-inks from high school | 1976.

Freedom. I was into hunting ducks back then, and my hero was Herb Jones, a painter of great talent who did watercolors of ducks and scenes that were reminiscent of where I lived, and the Tidewater area in general. So, I started doing watercolors and pen-and-ink drawings of ducks and geese. When I was done, I carried them down to the office and sold them to teachers and others in the office. As a senior, I ruled the hallways.

This, of course, bloated my artistic ego to the point that I thought I was hot stuff. I almost got a scholarship to VCU's art program, but my dad made too much money. Soon upon arrival, I realized that my art was not all that special, as there was a tremendous amount of talent out in the art world.

I worked hard to become a gifted illustrator. I was good, and sometimes gifted, but ultimately realized I probably could not make a living at it. So, I went into Communications Arts & Design, with the idea of becoming a graphic designer, where there were many more job opportunities than in fine arts and illustration.

After working in the advertising world for twelve years as an art director, I decided the time was right to start my own studio. So, I jumped on that crazy train, and we moved to Virginia Beach in 1994. That was the time that Apple released the QuickTake 100, the first digital camera. My favorite thing back then was to take pictures of friends and clients and then use Photoshop to place them in another background or turn them into a whale (or anything at all).

I became Photoshop King in the area and made a lot of money retouching and doing digital illustrations, using Photoshop and a Wacom tablet with a pressure-sensitive pen. The pressure sensitivity was a major breakthrough, allowing for huge advances in the art world.

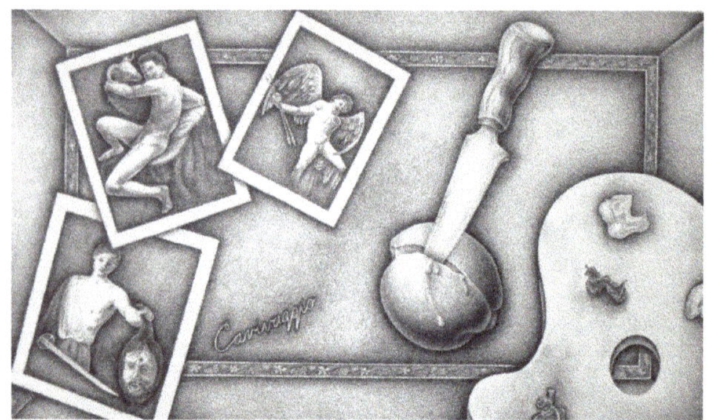

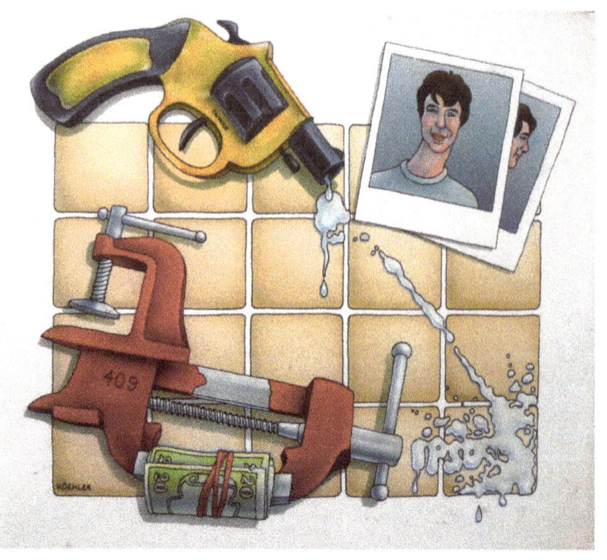

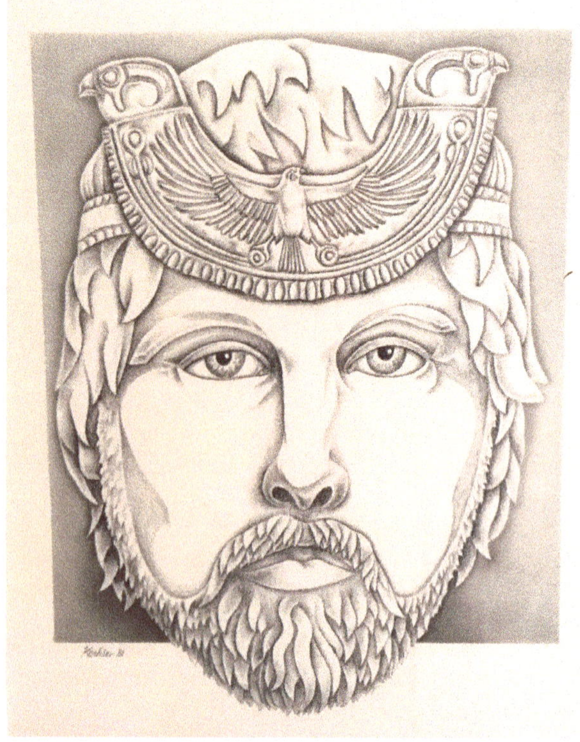

Illustration class projects at VCU | 1978-1980.

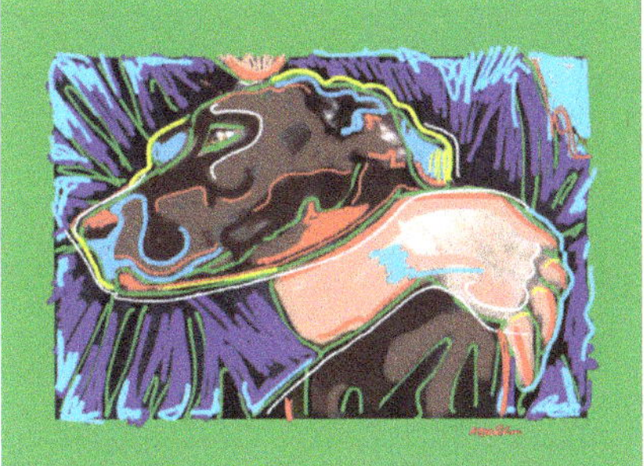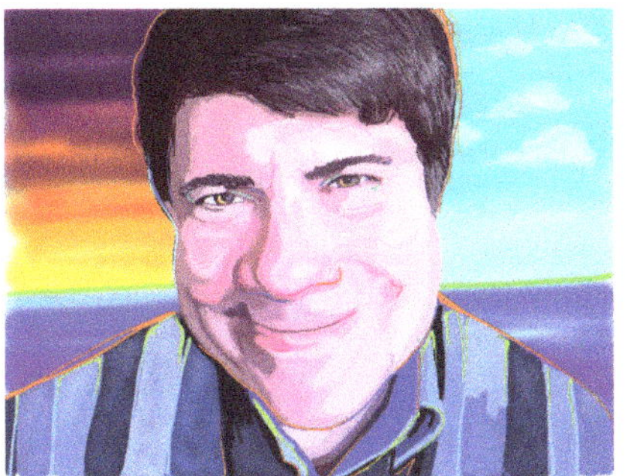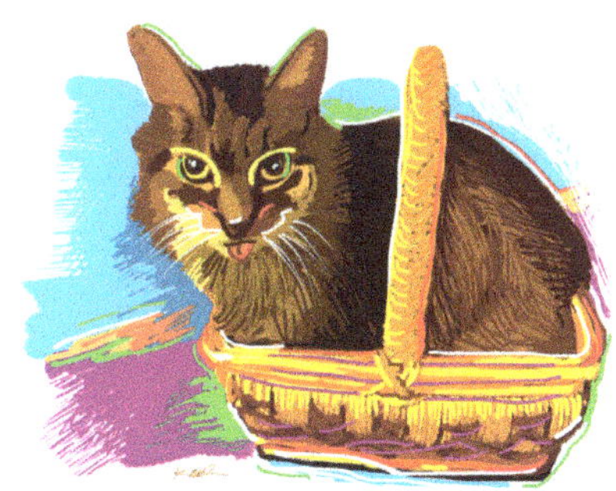

Three works done with Brushes finger painting app | 2011.

Fast-forward to 2010 when the first iPad was released. I made art using a program called Brushes with my finger. Who knew that finger painting would come back in style! The big breakthrough for me was that I was working directly on the *art* surface, like paper or canvas, but in a digital world. This made the creative process more intimate, and my canvas became mobile. I read books on my iPad and also created works of art.

Fast-forward again to 2018, when Apple released the iPad Pro with much higher resolution and responsiveness, along with the Apple Pencil. The Pencil is so much better than a Wacom tablet because it's directly in touch with the art surface (the glass face of the iPad), and the responsiveness is incredible. Plus, the huge range of brush tips, from calligraphic, airbrushing, drawing, crayon, oil painting, watercolor, textures, just about any kind of brush tip you can think of. Easy to experiment and change directions on the fly, not to mention undo and alter.

As with Photoshop, layering was a key element with ProCreate. Digital layers are like an old Disney animation, with cells layered on top of each other to get the final effect. The great thing about layers is that they can be removed, altered, or moved up or down. You can also create different effects with each layer by darkening, colorizing, and lightening them, or overlaying any number of effects that can be used or turned off quickly, giving the artist a diverse series of looks for the work.

This breakthrough in equipment and software made it super easy for me to simply create art. No pulling out the drawing pad or setting up an easel. No schlepping out to a beautiful spot, except to take a photo. It was easy, so I did it. It satisfied all my desires for ease of use and speed and offered me a huge range of options. At first, I was tentative and essentially retouched the photos I took. But over time, I began experimenting with bigger brushes to show the marks and become more expressive.

Strong color became my trademark. I experimented with color alterations and shifting colors to create effects. Eventually, it began to work, and some of my artist friends called me a *colorist*. I was cool with that, and I also found out that it is easy to shift from cool and amazing colors to too much color. Easy to overdo. Or sometimes not do enough. Still a learning experience.

As I had done way back in 1994, I began taking photos and doing digital portraits of friends and family who were willing to pose. I would take the chosen photo and remove the background, then paint and retouch, add a background, and off I went. I would usually give the person a print or even a framed canvas. Most of the time, they liked it, but sometimes, they did not, as I could be heavy-handed with my experimentation. All artists want to please others, but sometimes that is not possible, and only the artist is pleased.

I was asked to do some portraits for hire, but priced myself out of the market on purpose, because I did not feel I was ready, and did not want a client telling me to *smooth it out*, or *add red*, or *why did I make her nose green*. The commercial aspect interested me not. Maybe one day, but even then, I would insist on doing it my way—or the highway.

I would stare at that person for hours as I worked on their iPad portrait, so it was quite a lovefest while I studied all aspects of their face. That was the primary reason for creating the portraits. It was an act of love and friendship, a personal and very intimate gift that I could give. No different in essence from the QuickTake 100 portraits, just a lot closer.

Dogs have been a key part of my art development, as you will see. Max, the dog, and now Boomer, have posed for me countless times as they search the dunes for the elusive dune rats, or simply held still as I told them to SIT!

My grandkids Elijah and Lillian also provided me with countless photos that lent themselves to art projects. Using them as a basis for surrealistic images was a lot of fun and produced perhaps some of my best work.

Over the past few years, I have caught a little flak from some of my artist friends for not drawing from nature, aka plein air painting. I actually tried it a little but did not like it. Too slow. So much better to manipulate a photo that I took. After all, that is exactly what photographers do, and no one gives them flak. Ask my friend Glen McClure if he manipulates and does postproduction work on his photos. Of course, he does digital *dodging and burning* to lighten or darken, respectively. Begin with nature. Add artist.

So, for me, taking the photo was my plein air imagery, upon which I would paint. The photo itself is the realistic rendering upon which I added my layers of imagination to make it my own artistic expression.

My friend, the master artist and author Peter Bragino, says that an accurate rendering of a subject does not make it art, and that art is the expression of the subject by the artist to make it uniquely personal and different than the original rendering of reality. I tend to agree, but the illustrator and photo-retoucher in me might argue the point. A photo *is* a rendering, and some renderings transcend into art by their beauty and ability to capture the subject *as is*.

The photo paintings I have done typically take three to four hours, sometimes a bit less or more. Very fast compared to some artists, but I never liked the idea of taking days, weeks, or months on a piece of art. Yikes! I subscribe to the Vincent Van Gogh approach of working feverishly fast until exhausted by the work, at which point I would take a break to recover—until the next spell took me and I was off again on my next series. Vincent would often produce two to three paintings a day. My norm, with a full-time job, has been one piece a day.

My body of work since late in 2018 is about 350 pieces. I have narrowed those down for this book and for the show of my work to fewer than sixty works. Each is shown in one of five categories: dogs, grandkids, self-portraits, Lynnhaven River Series, portraits, and breakthrough.

The breakthrough art is both a revelatory moment of discovery for me and an apt description of the technique I have found. My work before proved my ability to render and create realism and surrealism from life using representational depictions of life.

The breakthrough moment came when I casually started layering multiple images in such a way as to create something unexpected, an abstraction of life, if you will. In other words, I did not set out to abstract as a conscious plan but stumbled into it by daydream wanderings. The word I used on that first piece was "Wow!" I continue to use that word quite a lot after creating over sixty pieces in this breakthrough style, because the many options of layering, color shifts, and filter options create literally thousands of options to experiment with, an artistic Rubik's cube of possibilities.

AND NOW . . . THE ART.

DOGS

I have had dogs as pets for most of my life. They have been a large part of my life, and for the most part, I never looked at them in an artistic way—until 2018. We had a foster dog named Max. He was rather striking looking, with a curled-over, husky tail, blue-black body, with tan and white markings. He was visually interesting, and I noticed.

I began taking photos of him at the beach and reworking the image. Then I started making patterns with him flying on the page and doing various things. Kind of a Warhol look.

Earlier in 2022, we picked up a chocolate lab puppy we named Boomer, who, at ten months, weighs about eighty pounds. So much for the idea of getting a small dog. Once again, I began taking photos of Boom dog.

The pieces I am showing are often about repeating patterns using color as an adjunct, with some of the images becoming rough mandalas and wallpaper.

People love dogs, and my best-selling piece by far has been *Max in Flight*. For the most part, I do not create art to sell, but instead create art I like, and if it sells, then *mazel tov* and amen. Many fine artists create what they think will sell,

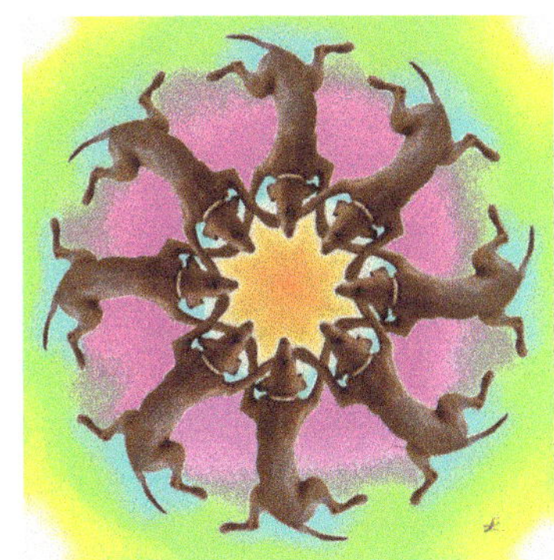

Boomer Mandala #2 | 2021

which some say pushes them into the commercial arena. But I'm cool with it all, and if something sells or does not, then no worries either way. "Can't buy me love," as the song says.

I also created patterns with dogs to infuse a somewhat Escher-like feel to the pieces. And of course, once I started putting them in a circle, very cool patterns emerged, and some mandalas were born.

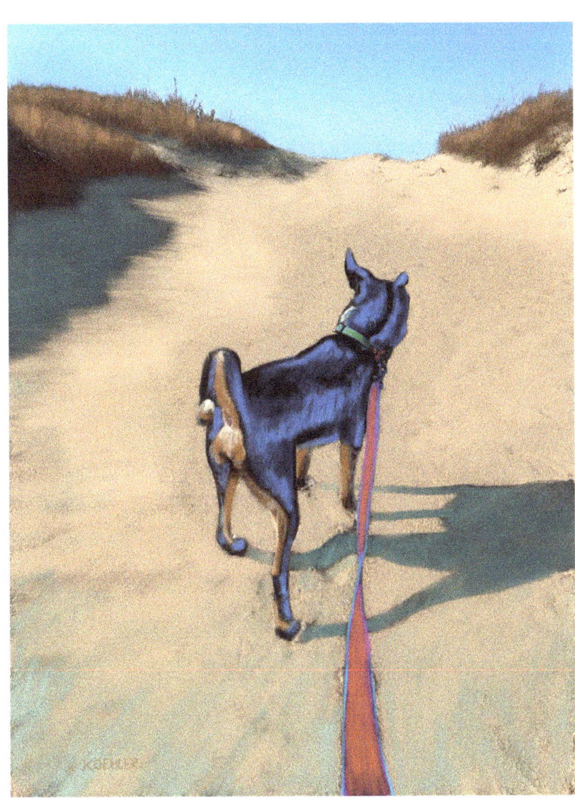

Looking for Dune Rats | 2019

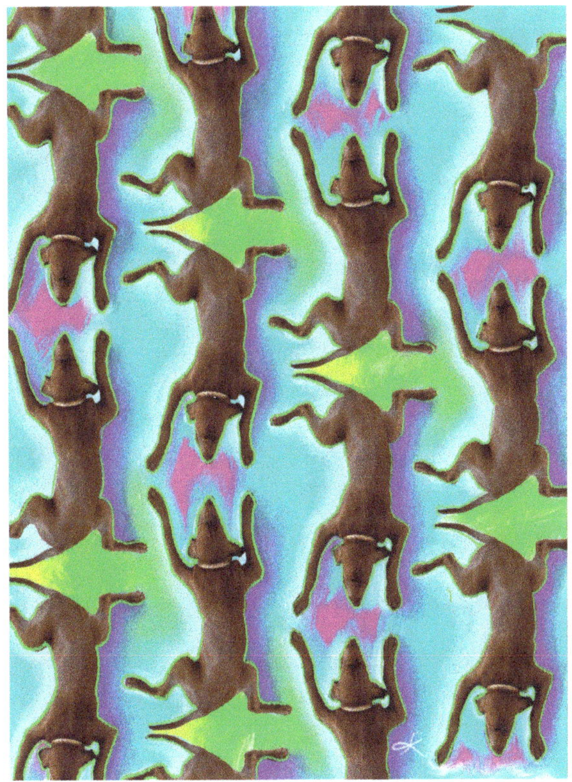

Pointing Boomer | 2021

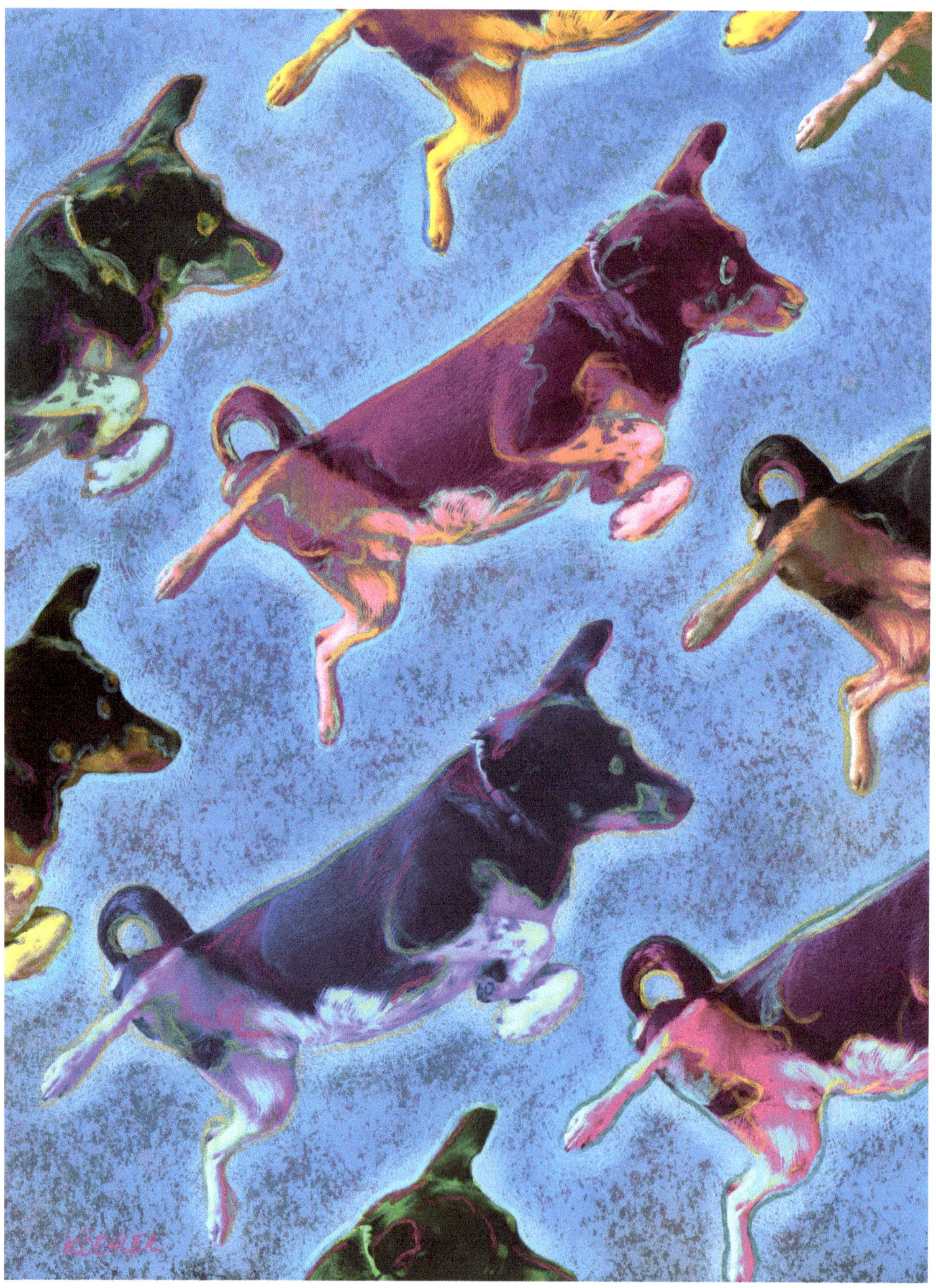

Max in Flight | 2020

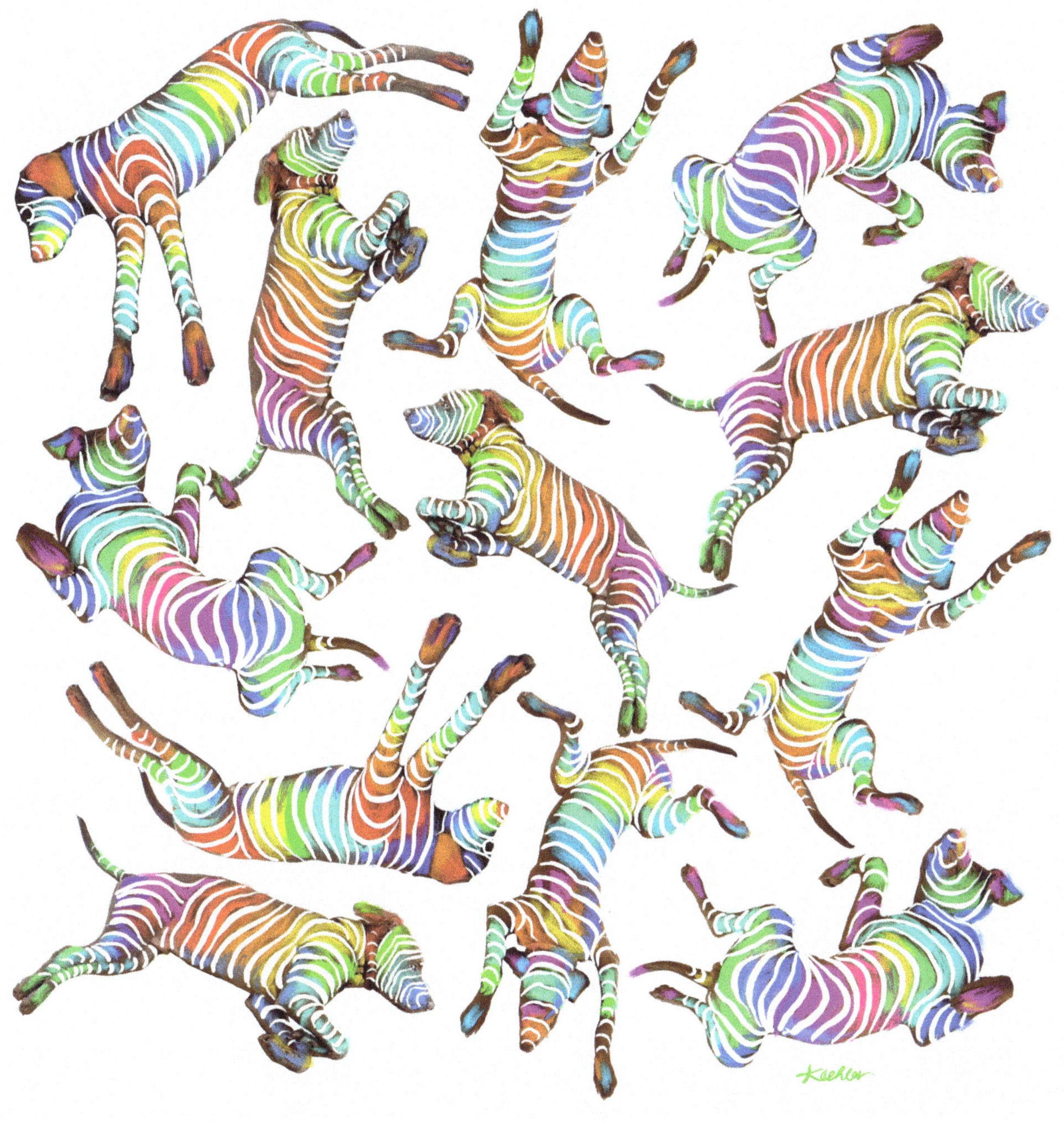

Flying Kudu Dogs | *2021*

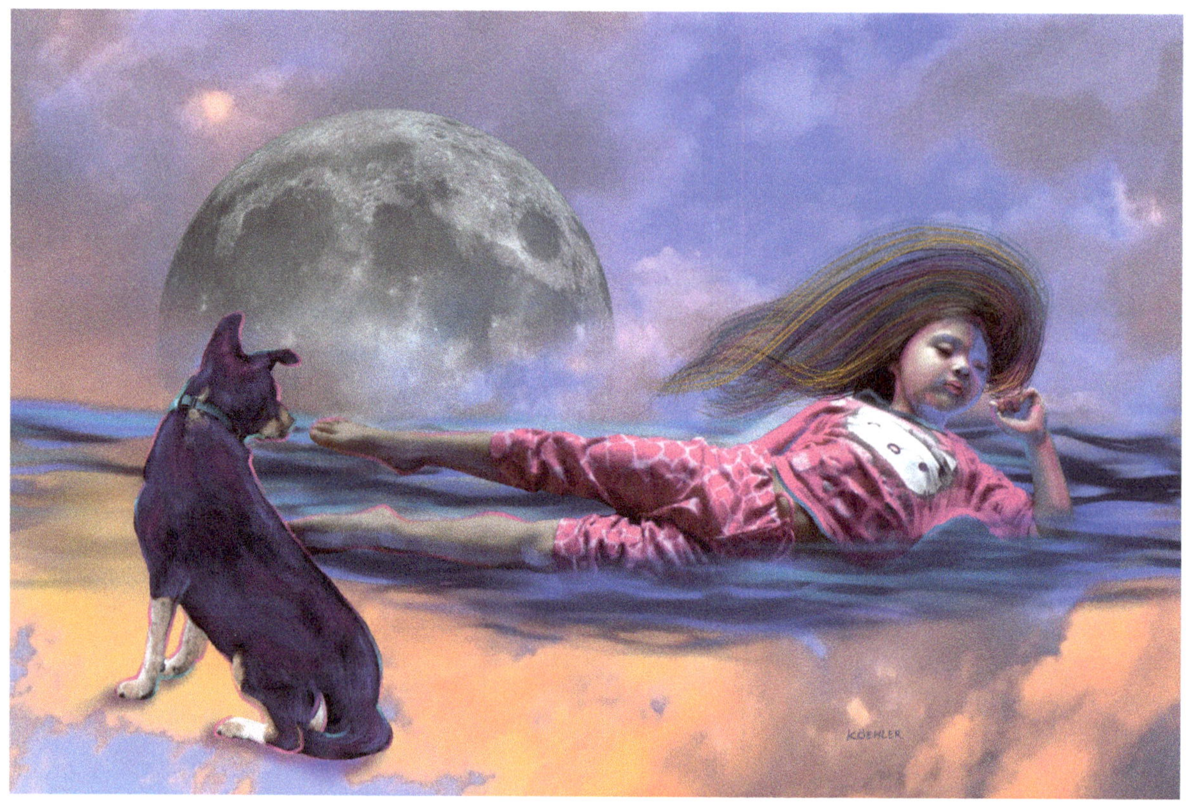

Dreaming of Moon & Dog | 2019

GRAND KIDS

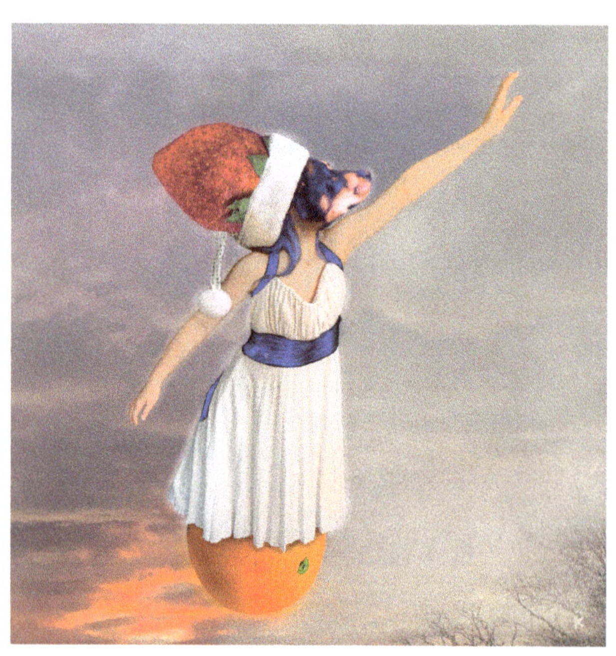

Clearing the Sky | 2019

The first image I did in this series was from a photo of Lilli sleeping on top of her bedcovers. The kids lived with us for about six years, and most nights, I would kiss them goodnight (again) before I went up to bed. I kept coming back to that photo of Lilli and was delighted to turn it into *Dreaming of Moon and Dog*. It won an award at a local art show.

Later, I began combining photos of the kids with Max the dog in surrealistic ways. These were of course takeoffs from Magritte, the master of surrealism. Often, I used found objects or stock photos to help tell the story.

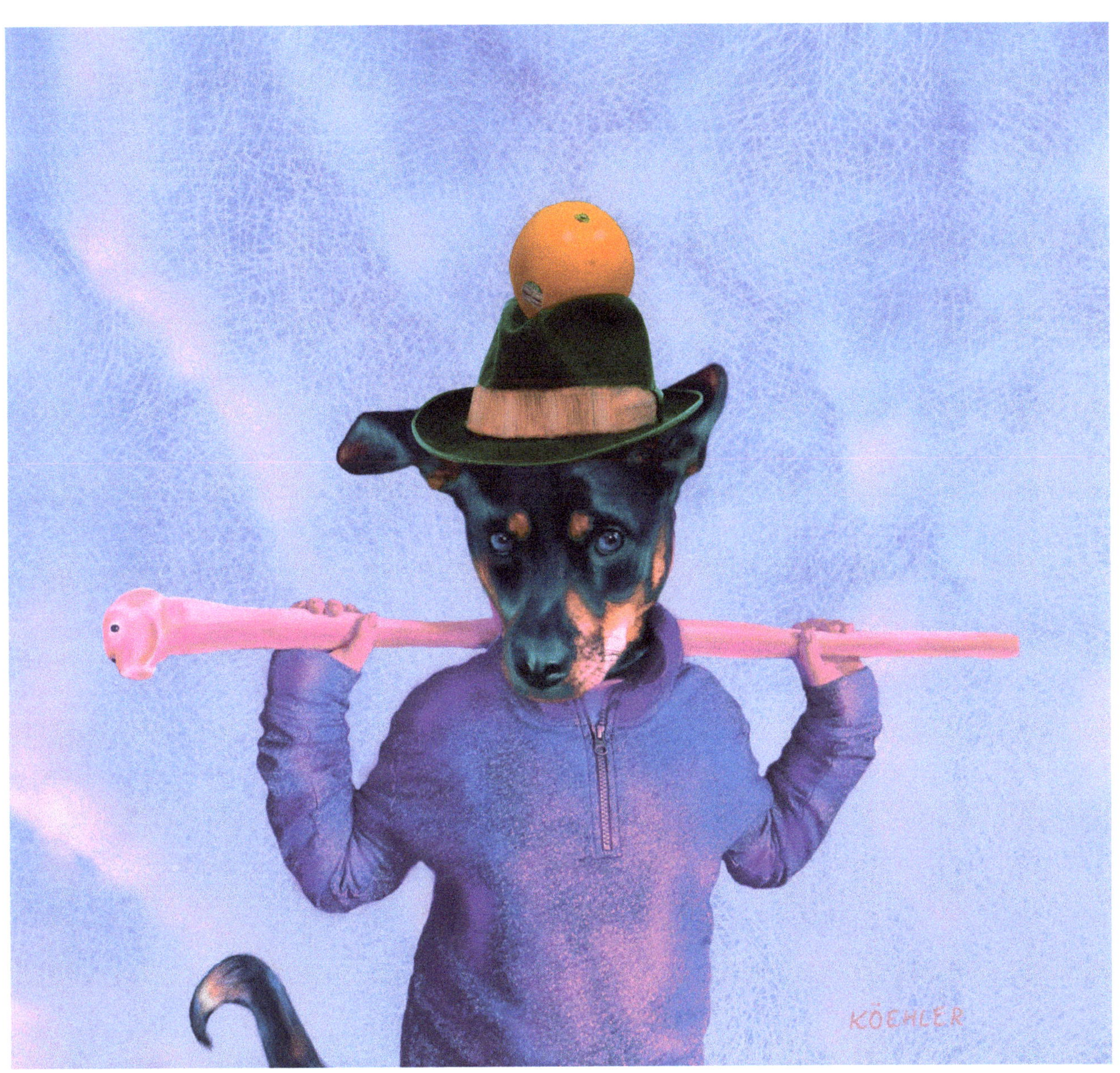

Elijah Max | 2019

PORTRAITS

I realize that there can be a certain level of conceit suggested by an artist who does as many self-portraits as I have. I admit to having an interest in depicting myself in various ways, but mainly I chose myself because I was always available. Plus, my modeling fees were quite reasonable.

I used myself as a model at first to sort out the techniques I hoped to develop. Initially, I was rather tame and mild-mannered, with the resulting work looking more like bad retouch than actual art. But that forced me to loosen up and go heavier with the paint application. If you are a traditional painter, you are probably thinking, *Ha, that's not real paint!* I would say that is true in the physical sense, but the virtual paint, colors, brushes, lines, and textures I use are very real. And as you can see for yourself, the technique is sometimes indistinguishable from physical paintings. Furthermore, the medium and method used by an artist should not determine the value of the art in any way.

I was more willing to experiment with self-portraits than I was with portraits of others. Take for instance the Linear John piece. I had wondered what it would be like to contour lines on a subject—in this case, a face. On a layer just about the photo, I drew the white contour lines, then I painted under the lines. Then I removed the photo and added a background layer on the bottom. Voilà! Sometimes cool things happen with little effort, and sometimes, after great effort, there is a dead end. Such is life.

After I had done several self-portraits, I figured it was okay for me to rock some portraits for friends and family. At first, I would say they did not rock so much as rolled, in a tepid way. I was timid and uncertain at first and essentially did retouching of the subjects. That is not such a bad thing in terms of cleaning up the person and accentuating the positive.

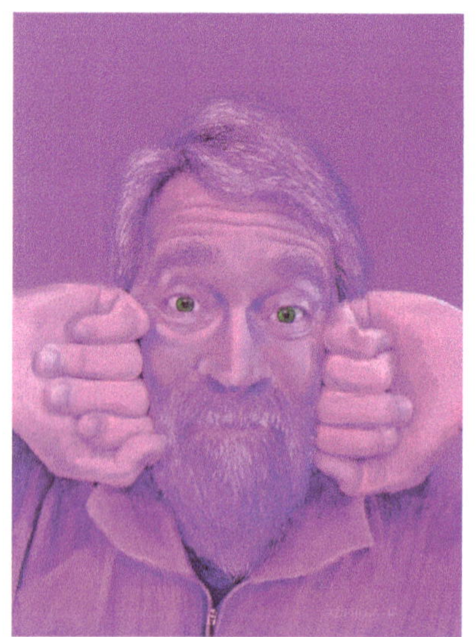

Purple John | 2019

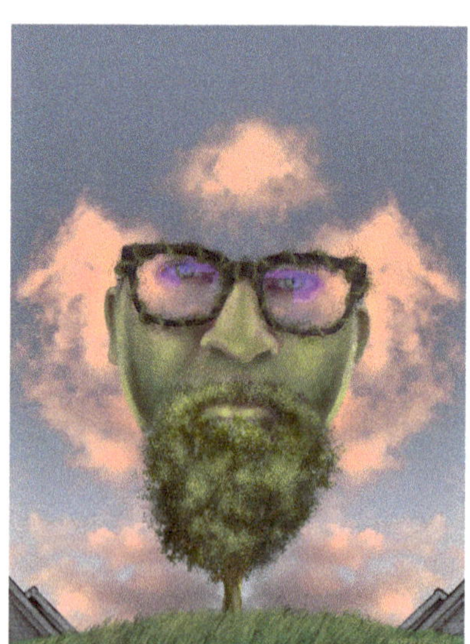

John Einstein | 2020

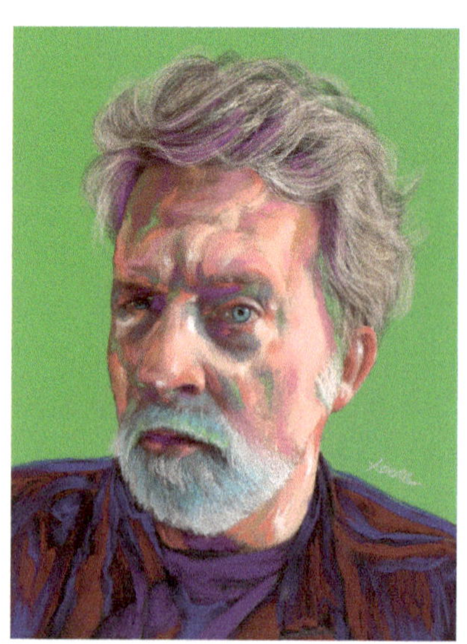

John Van Gogh | 2021

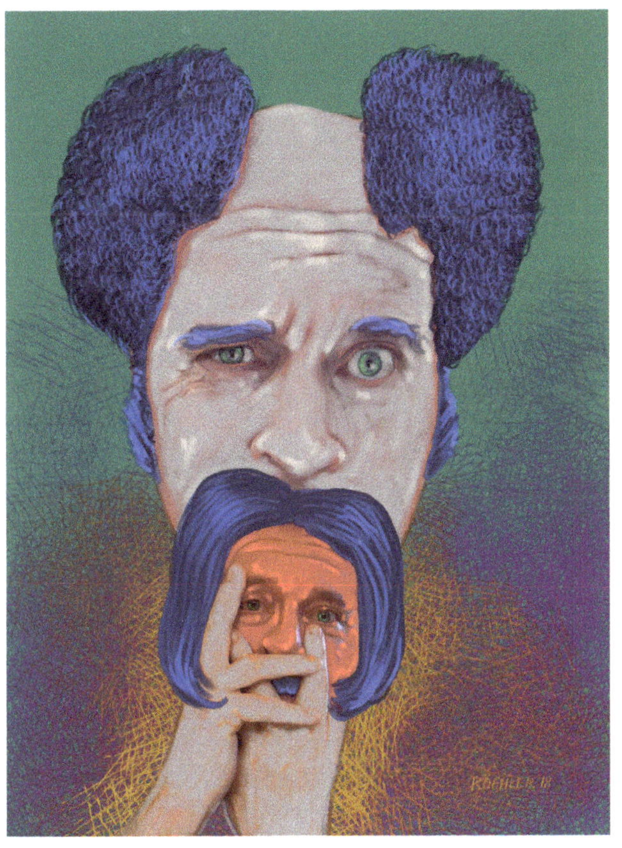

Double Clown | 2020

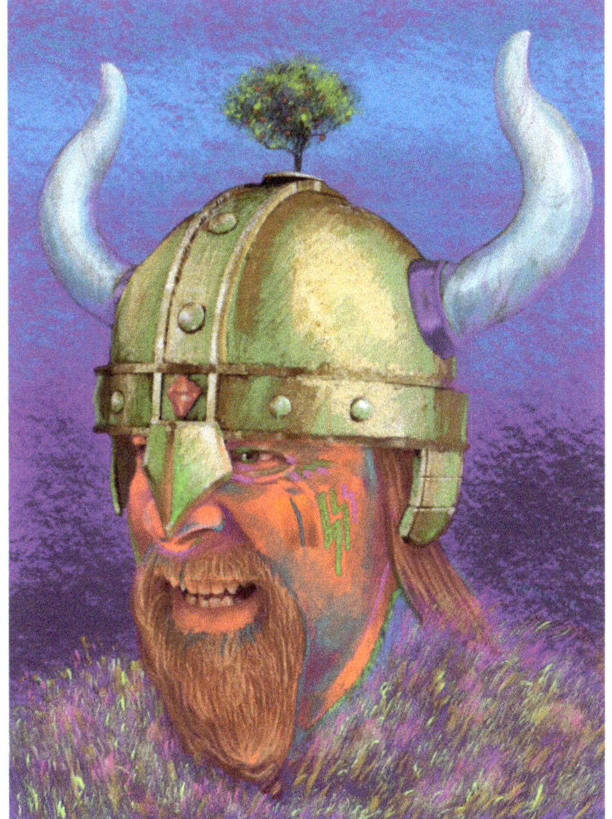

Viking John | 2019

I quickly realized I was doing renderings again—not art. So, I concentrated on developing a style that was more artistic and expressive, using larger brushes, broadcasting thicker strokes and stronger color application. Often, I would use bright primary or complimentary colors to add fluid movement and drama to the portraits. This could be deliciously successful or dismally awful. But if you are not prepared to fail artistically (as in life), you will never succeed.

The problem was that sometimes what I thought was fantastic did not exactly cause the person to jump for joy when they saw the finished piece. In pleasing myself, I did not always please the person whose portrait I was painting. Such is art.

I did the portraits as a gift for the person in the painting, and as a way to improve my art through trial and error. I only offered to do one for people I liked, because I knew I would be spending quite a bit of time with them, first with a series of photos from which I would pick, then several hours where I was painting intimately on their face, sometimes quite close. It was strangely an act of love that helped me to know them ever better.

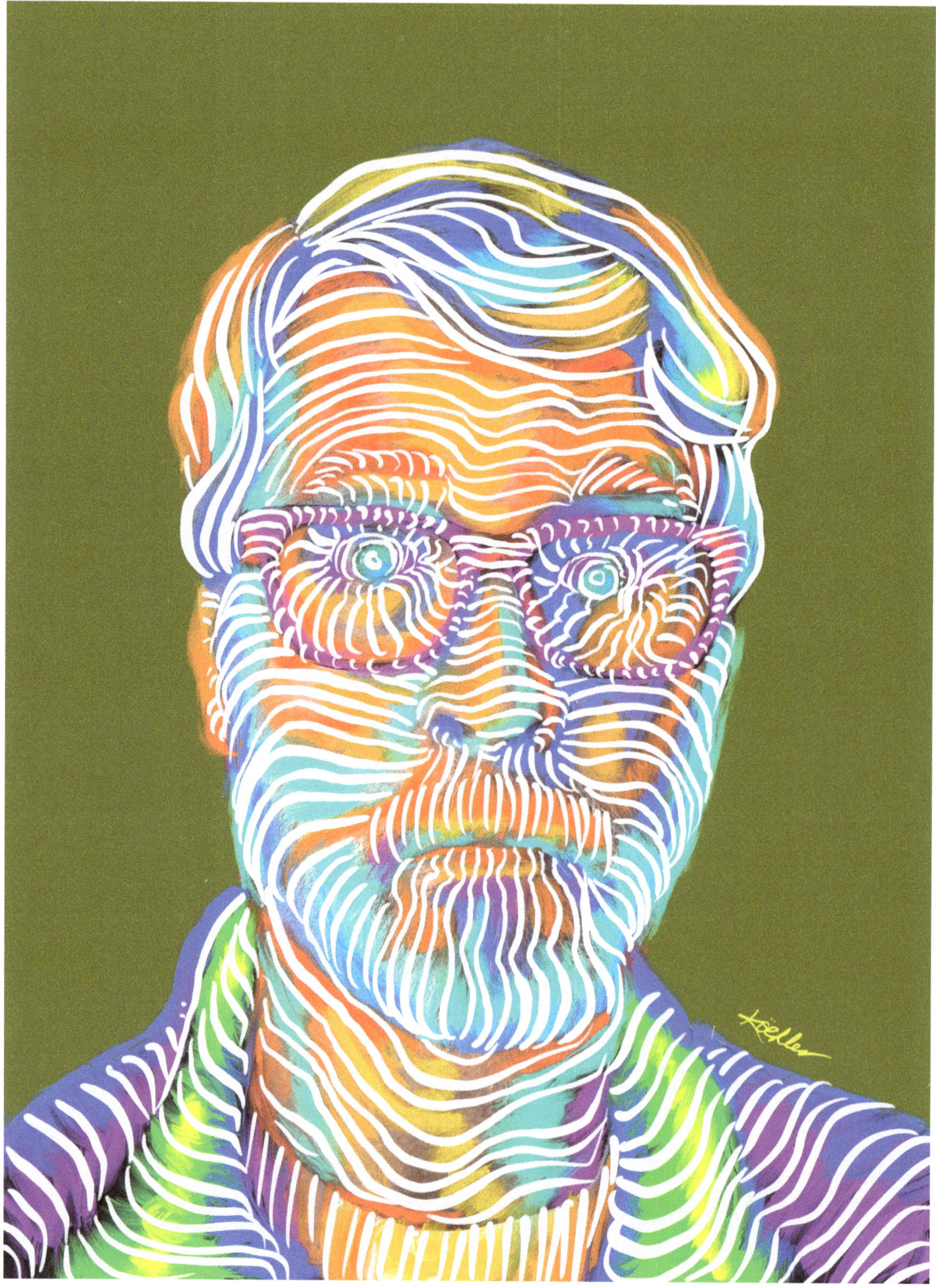

Topographically John | 2021

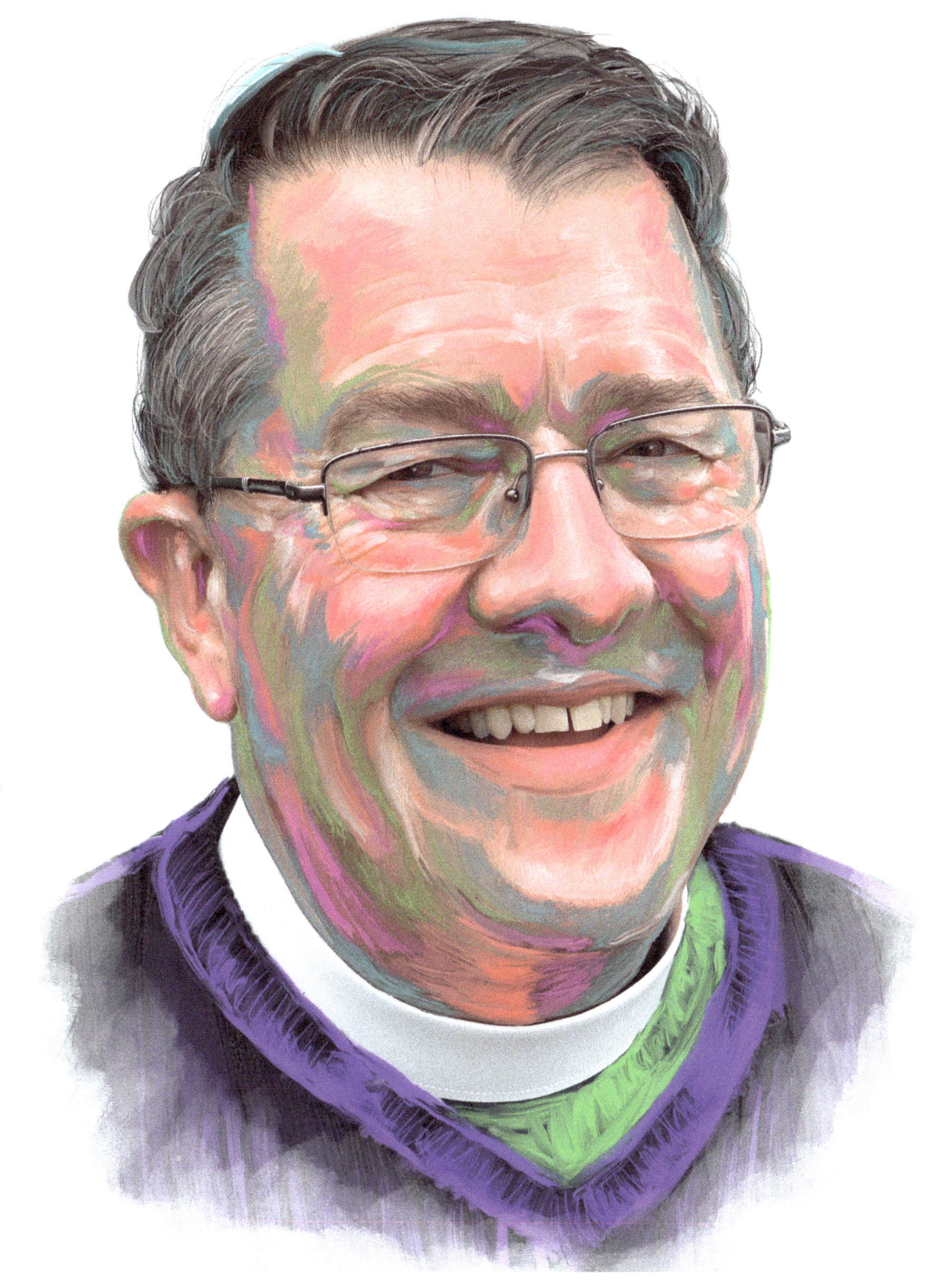

Rev. Nigel Mumford | 2020

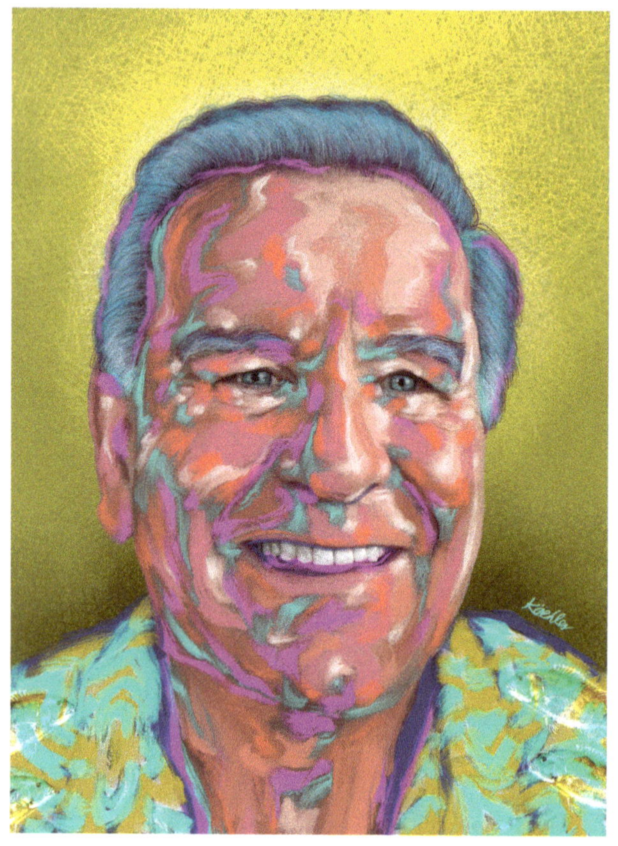
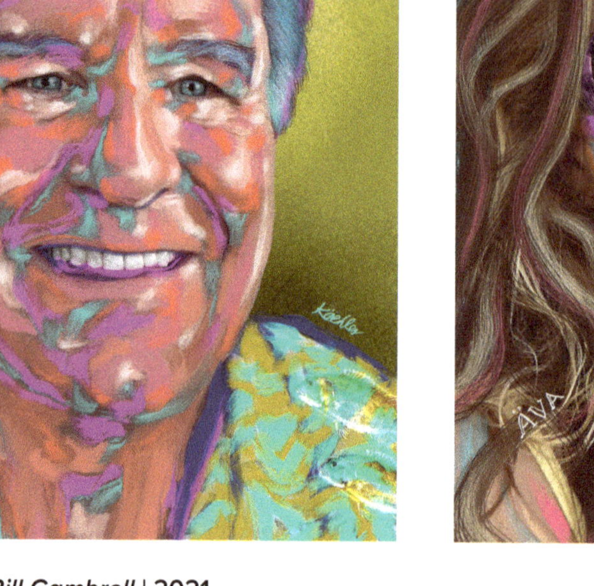

Bill Gambrell | 2021

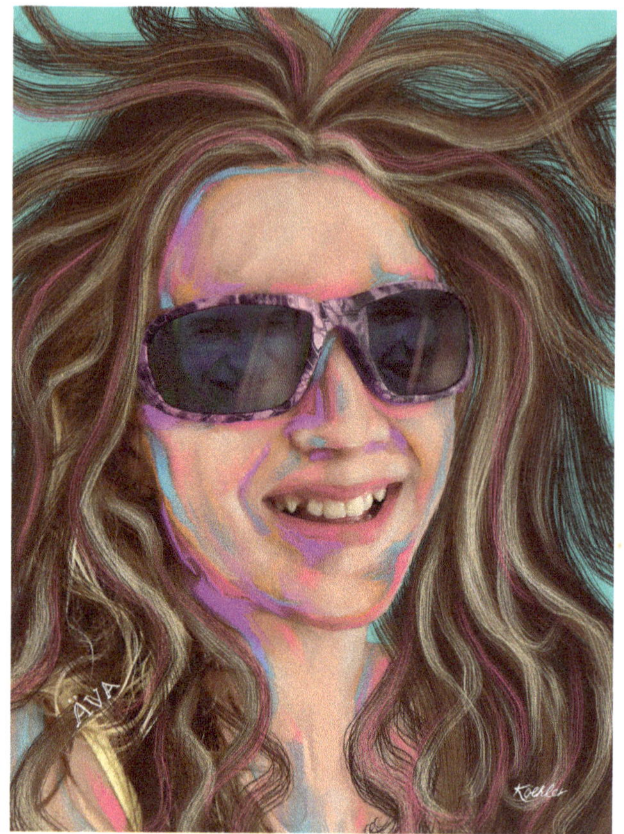

Ava Rollins | 2021

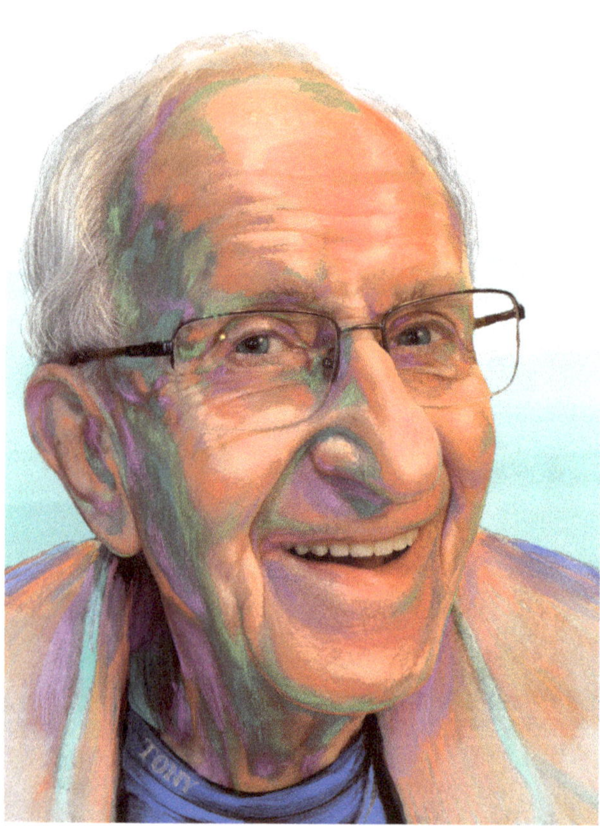

Dr. Tony Bruder | 2020

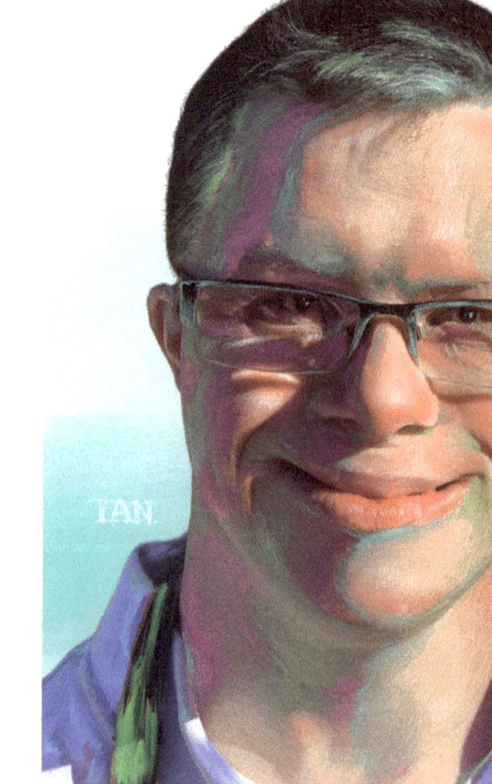

Ian | 2020

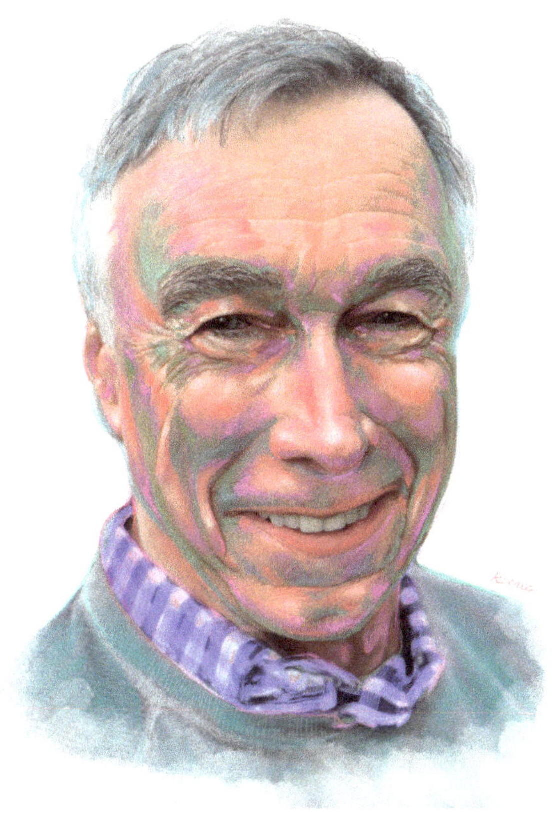

Bill Campbell | 2020

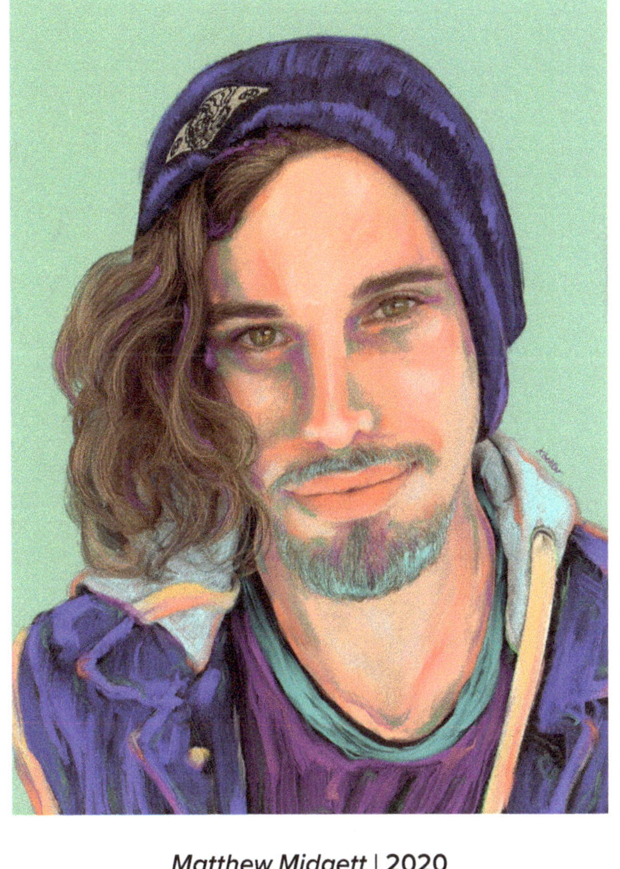

Matthew Midgett | 2020

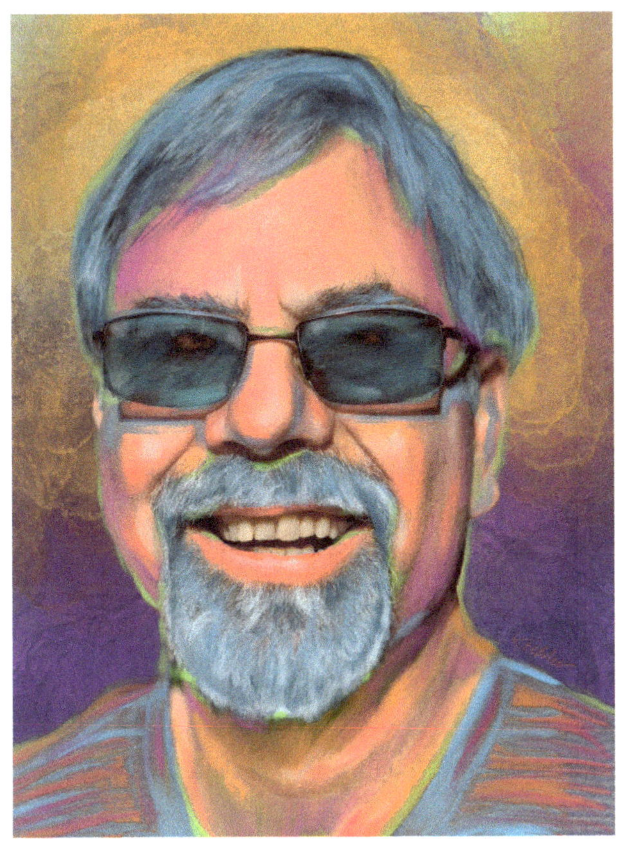

David Saile | 2020

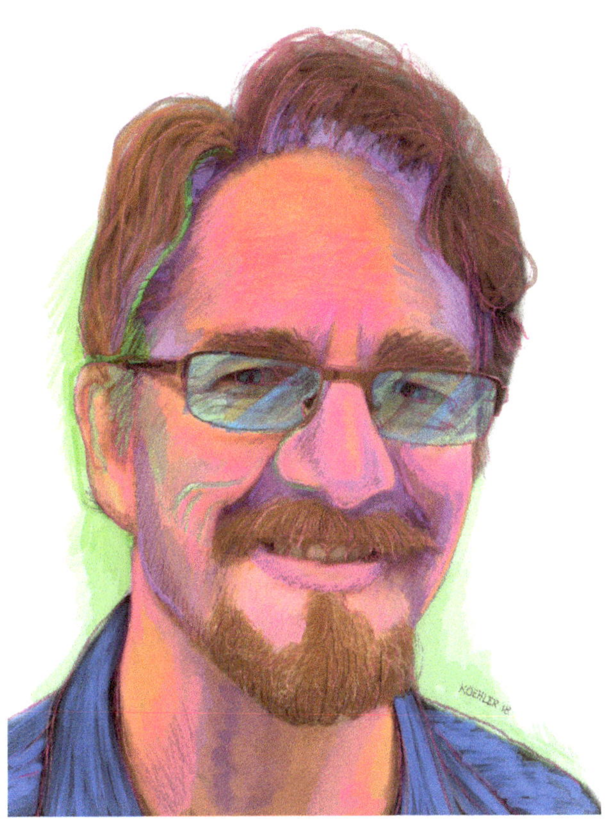

Mark Miltz | 2019

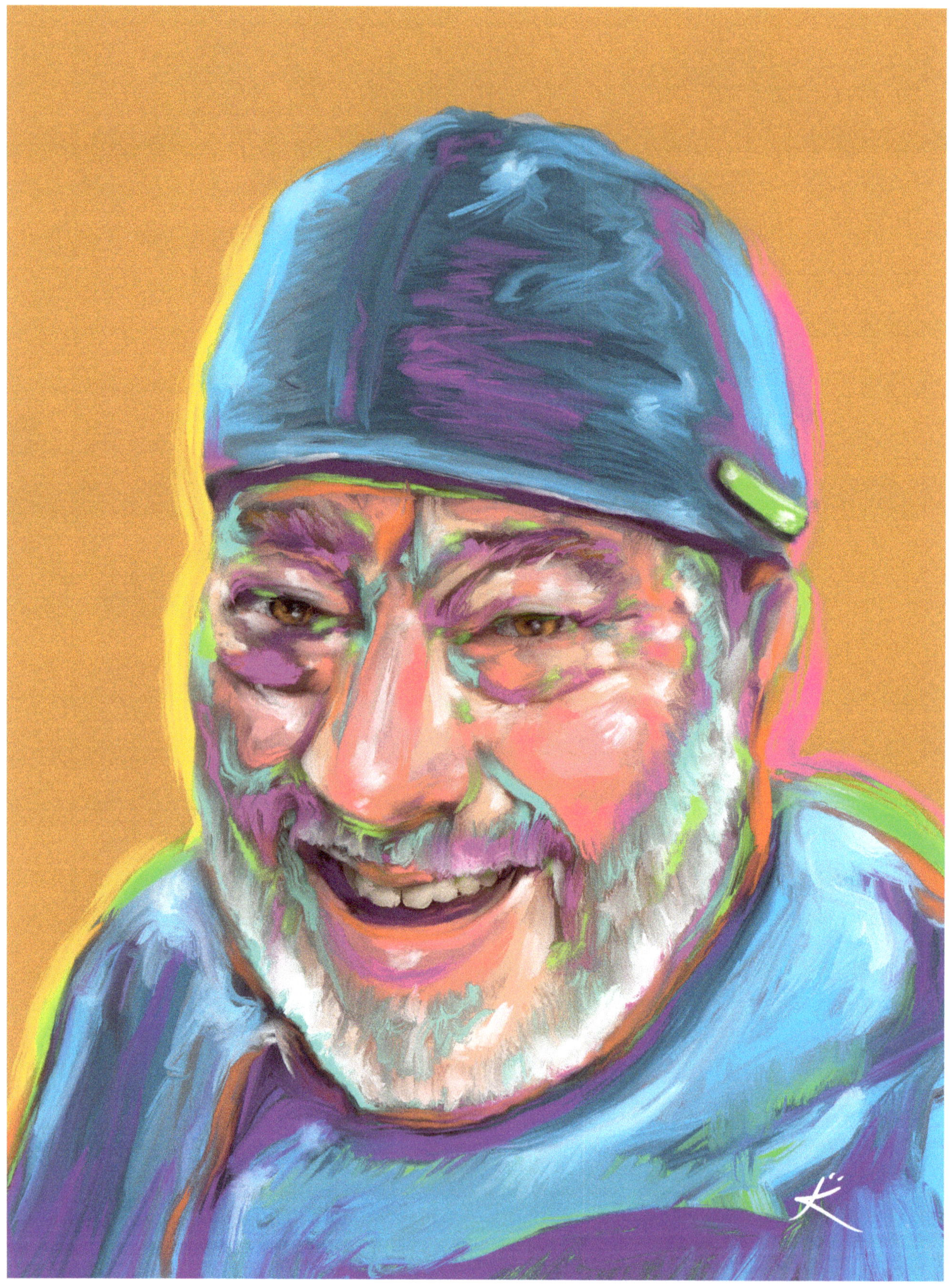

Dave Wilberger | 2021

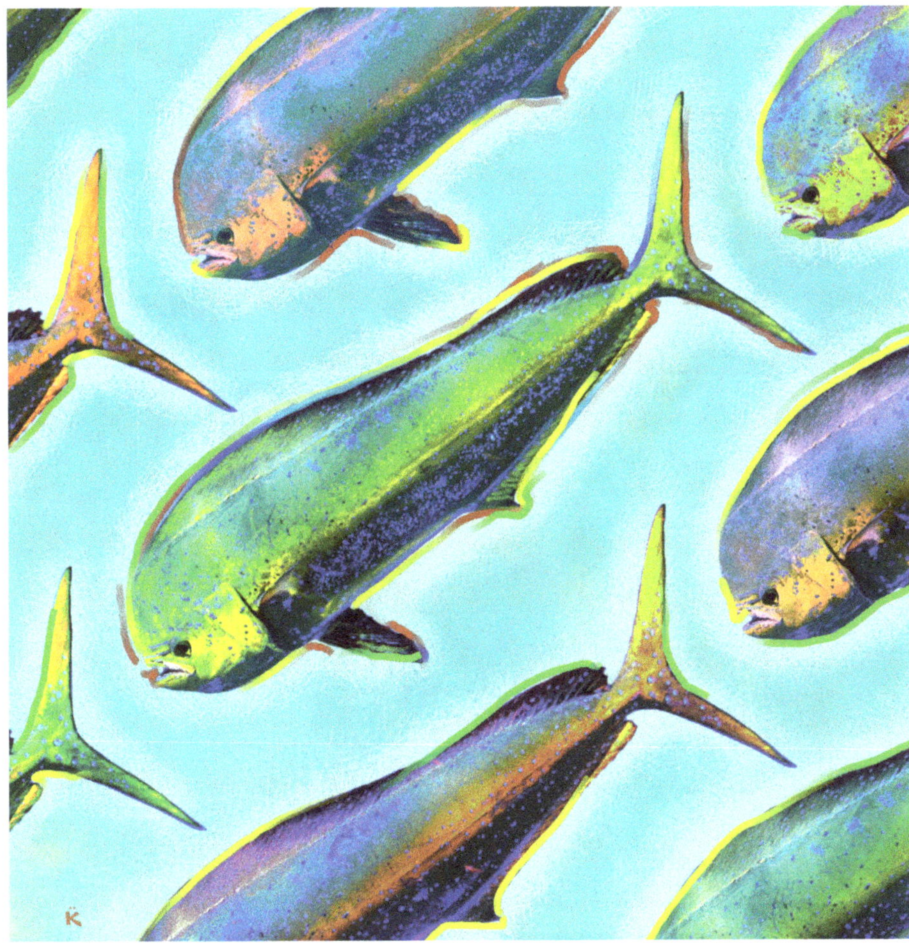

Mahi Mahi | 2020

LYNNHAVEN RIVER SERIES

I was looking for a new series of subjects, and my wife, Patty, suggested doing various Lynnhaven River animals. Perhaps this was something that could help raise money for the Lynnhaven River Project?

The crab was the first piece I did. I liked it and quickly knocked off a total of fourteen. I confess that they are more like illustrations than artworks. I also hoped that they would sell and was attempting to do pieces that folks would like. I managed to get some in a local gallery and sold a few. Like many of my art series, it was a learning process and a way to express myself.

This, then, is a conundrum for artists: should you create work that is suited to the buyers, or do the work you want to do without concern for the buyers? I don't always know the answer, but I can say that my art that sold or won awards was created more for my own personal enjoyment, and without thought or concern about whether folks would like it or not.

Even now, I look at those pieces that won or sold and wonder if I should do more like them. An artistic conundrum if ever there was one. Also, many would argue that illustration is art, but others would argue it is not fine art, that is a personal expression by the artist that transcends life in a meaningful way.

I think illustration is art. Period.

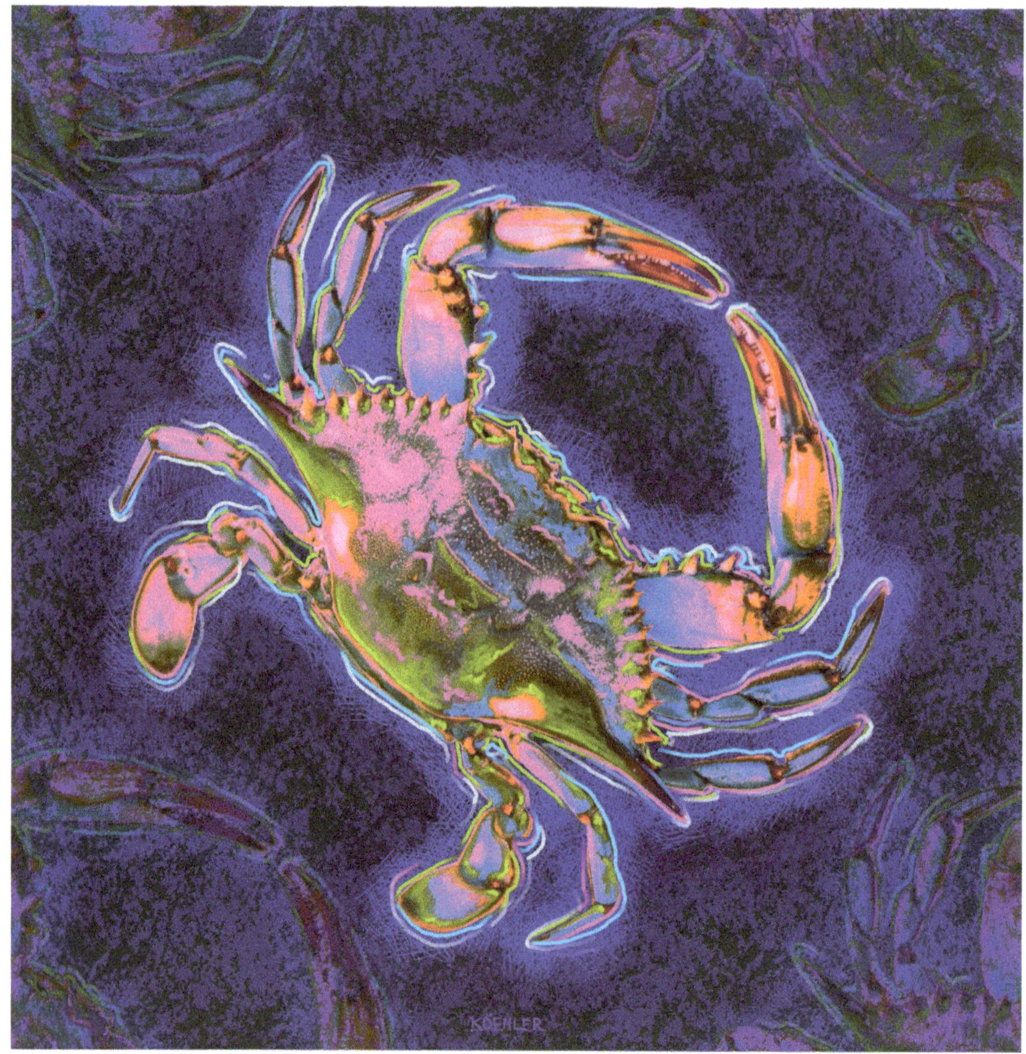

Blue Crab | 2020

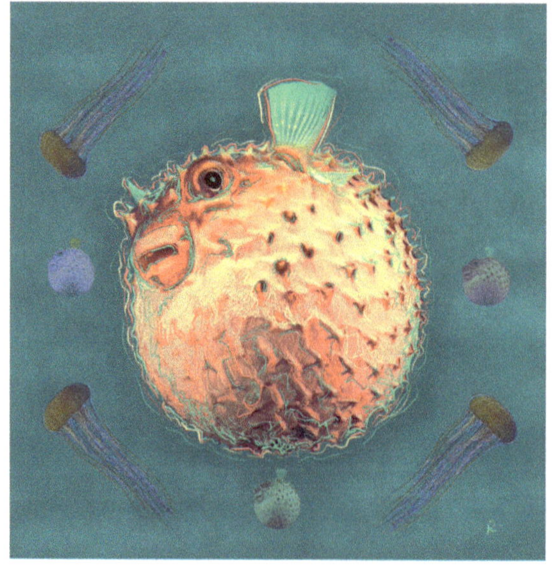

Blowfish | 2020

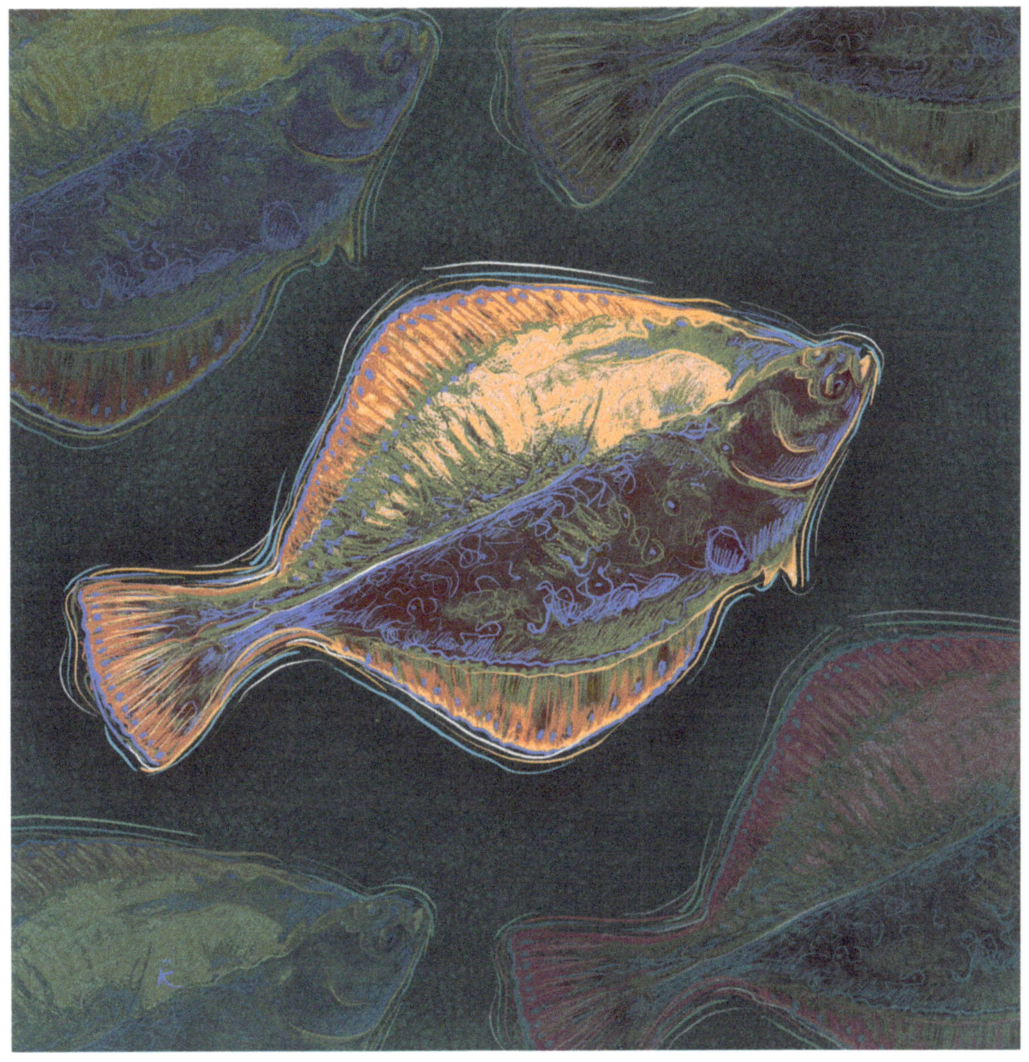

Flounder | 2020

WATER & EARTH

One day, around our pool, I thought it would be cool to do something with mermaids. I was told that mermaids are popular. Gosh, that sure is a reason to create art! Still, I liked the idea, so I bought a mermaid tail and hired our local ballerina, Rebecca Morgan Ailstock, a former neighbor, to pose for me. Ballerinas are amazingly capable of expressing themselves and life through their bodies. Priceless.

I also got my granddaughter, Lilli, involved and did some pieces of them together. My favorite is with the two mermaids swimming with the blue shark. I trended toward photorealism with these pieces, in a natural, yet surrealistic, way. I'm not sure why, but perhaps I wanted the realism to rule the day, and I did not want to express myself through brush strokes.

Surrealistic moments occurred in early 2022, when I took one of the nude images where she was falling back as if she had been pushed and added a mermaid tail and a beach scene with dunes, water, and sky elements. The key was that I experimented with layer effects, to create a dreamlike surrealism, in a piece titled *Water Birth* (see page 30). Negative imagery, photos blended in unusual ways. It was as if all my study blended with my dreams and imagination. The work seemed to resonate with viewers more than

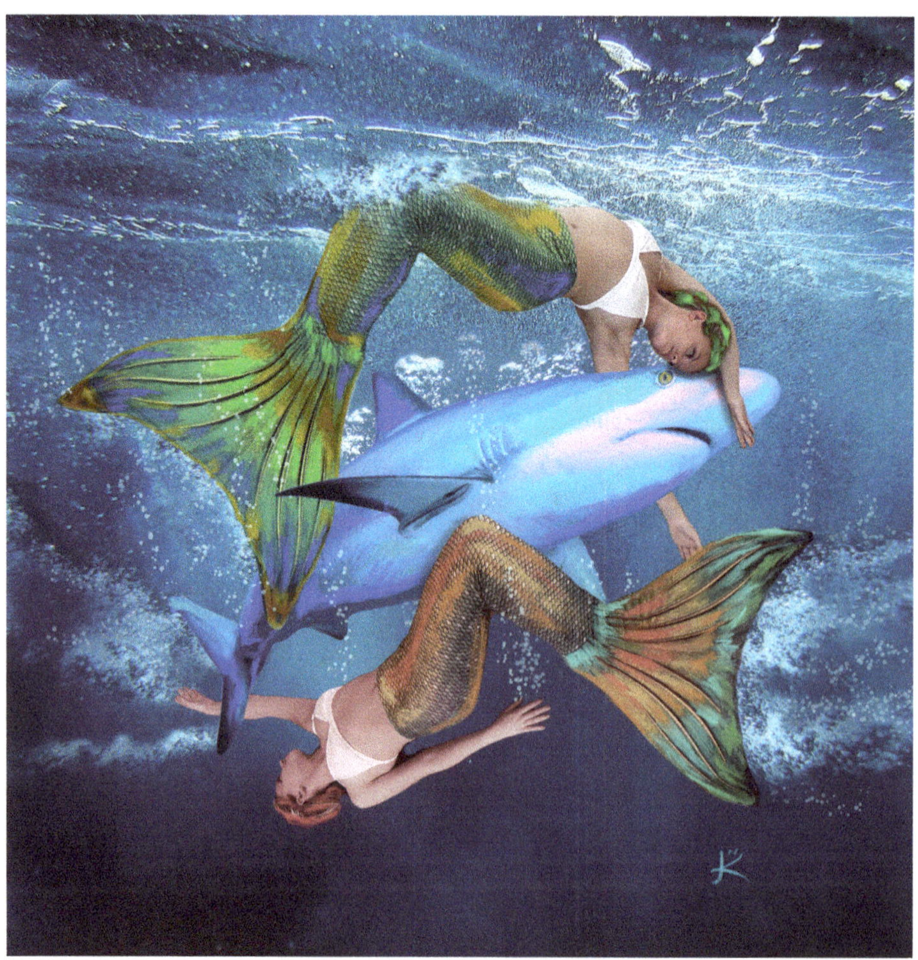

Dancing With the Blue Shark | 2021

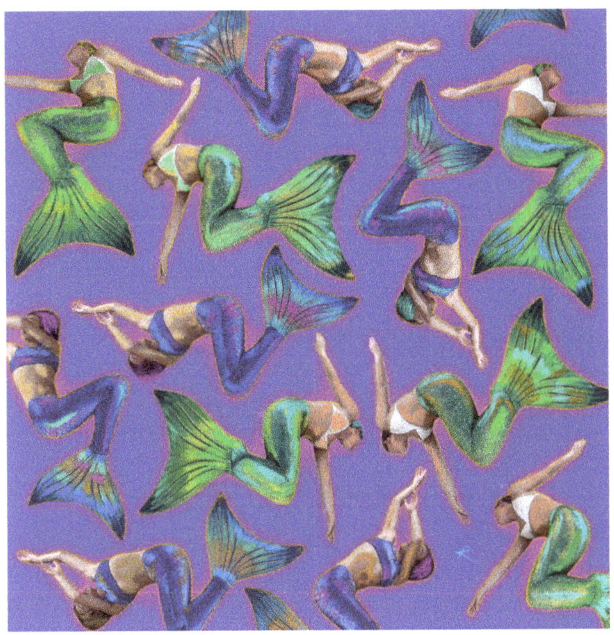

Mermaid Wallpaper | 2021

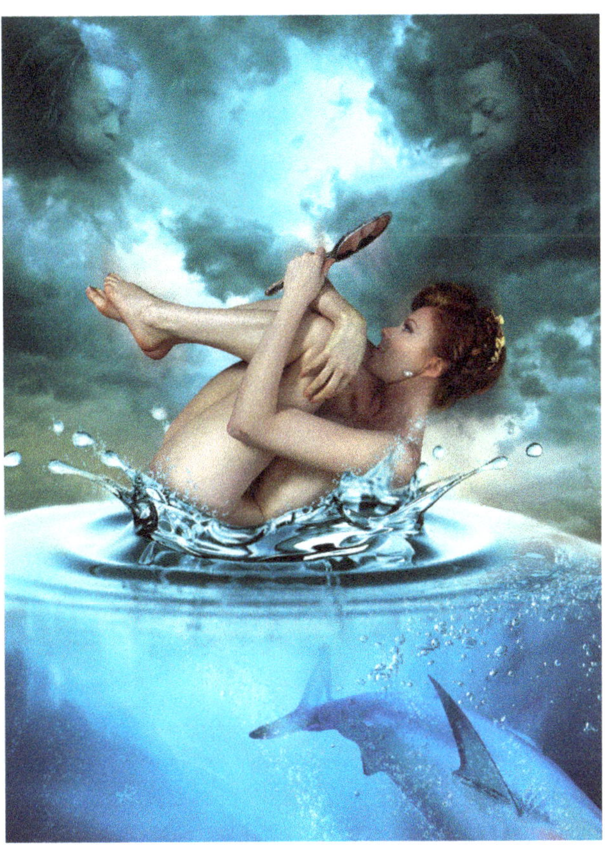

Adoration of the Mermaid | 2021

other recent work—and I liked the process. So, I did two more, and here we are.

In some cases, those moments were accidental, as it was with the piece *Dreams of the Mother.* Rebecca Morgan was laying on the log, and I noticed the branches below her looked like her legs. So, I removed her body, and there you have it.

I created the mermaid pieces to fulfill the specs for a show called H2O at the Virginia Beach Art Center. Unfortunately, their website did not accept my submissions, and I could not show the work. I was pretty upset, but they would not allow any kind of special dispensation since the judging had just been done. Bummer!

Rebecca Morgan also modeled for another series I did, and ultimately showed three in the From the Earth show at the VB Art Center. We went into the woods, and she posed on logs and trees in First Landing State Park. Our plan was to have her pose and unite with the natural forms, and then later I would manipulate,

colorize, and layer them on other objects. Once again, the idea of "found objects" came into play, with a digital twist. As I took the photos, I was not exactly sure how I would render them or what would happen. That mystery was a lot of fun. After I submitted the three to the Earth show, *Dreams of the Mother* was chosen for the VB Art Center show poster. Cool.

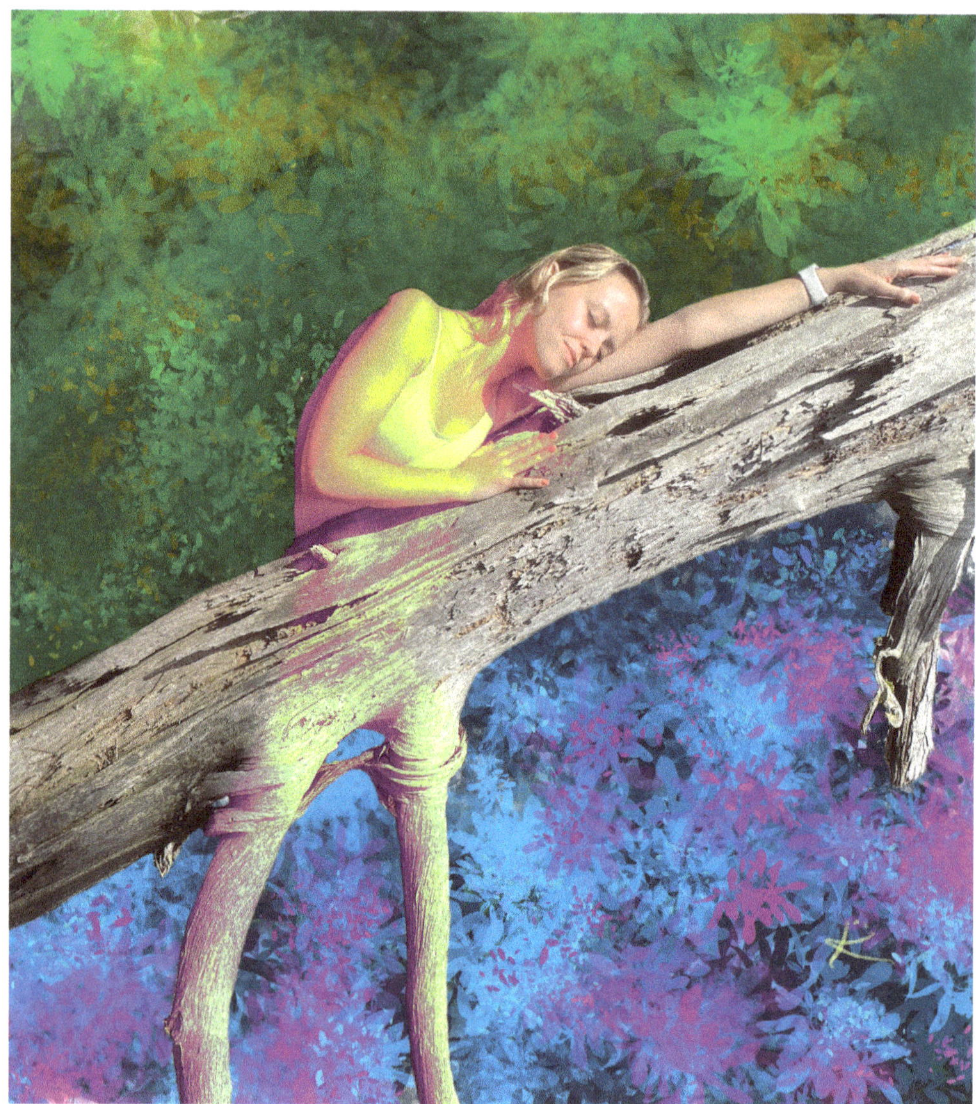

Dreams of the Mother | 2021

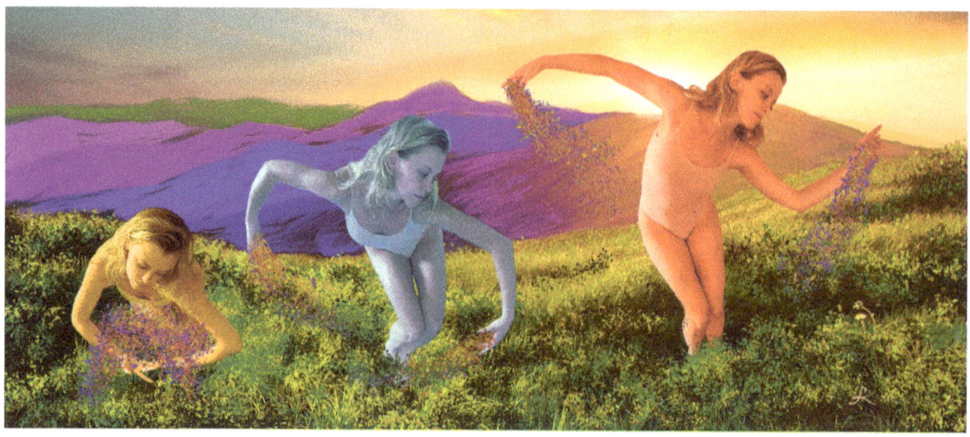

Dance of the Seasons | 2021

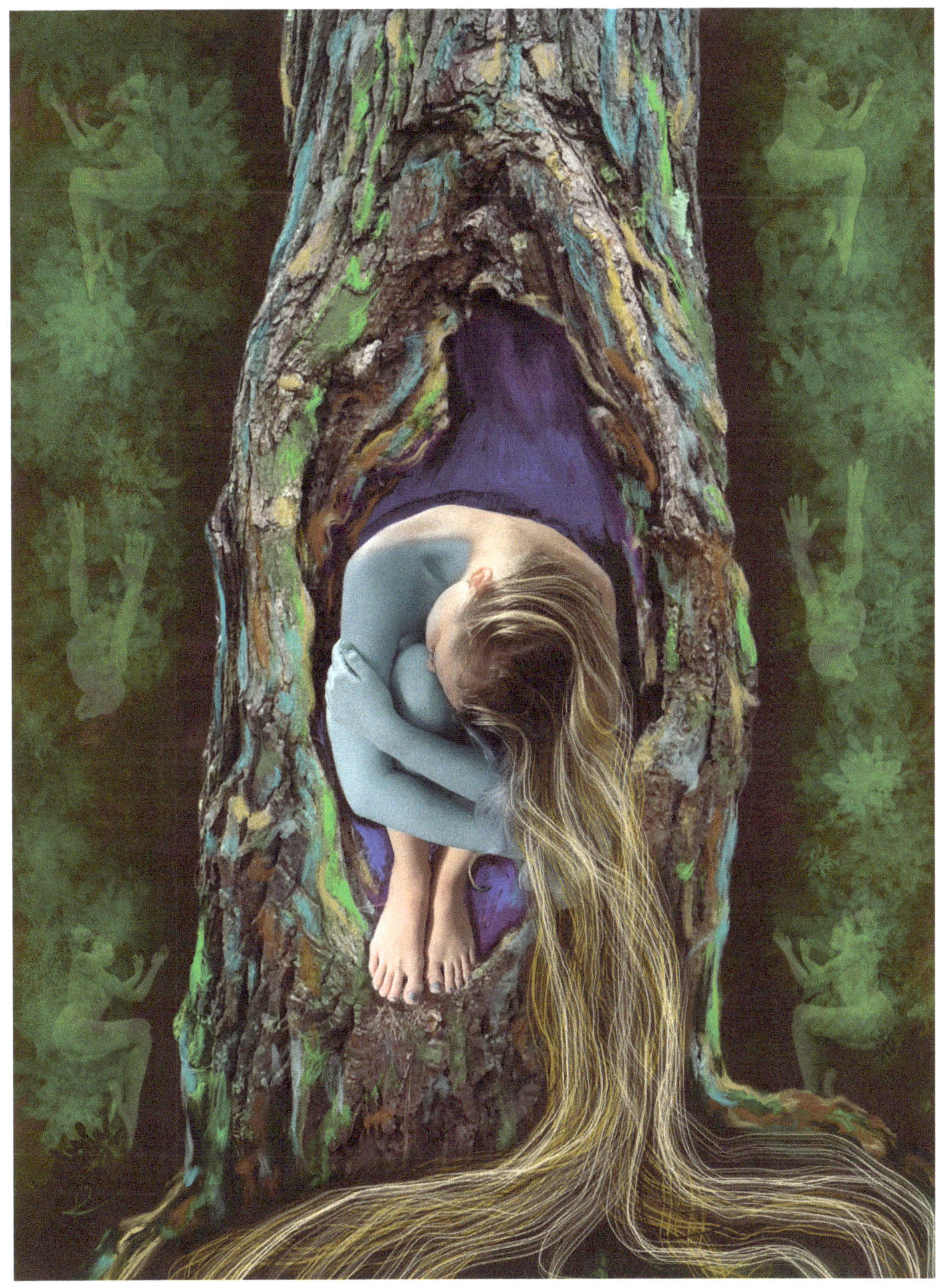

The Tree of Life | 2021

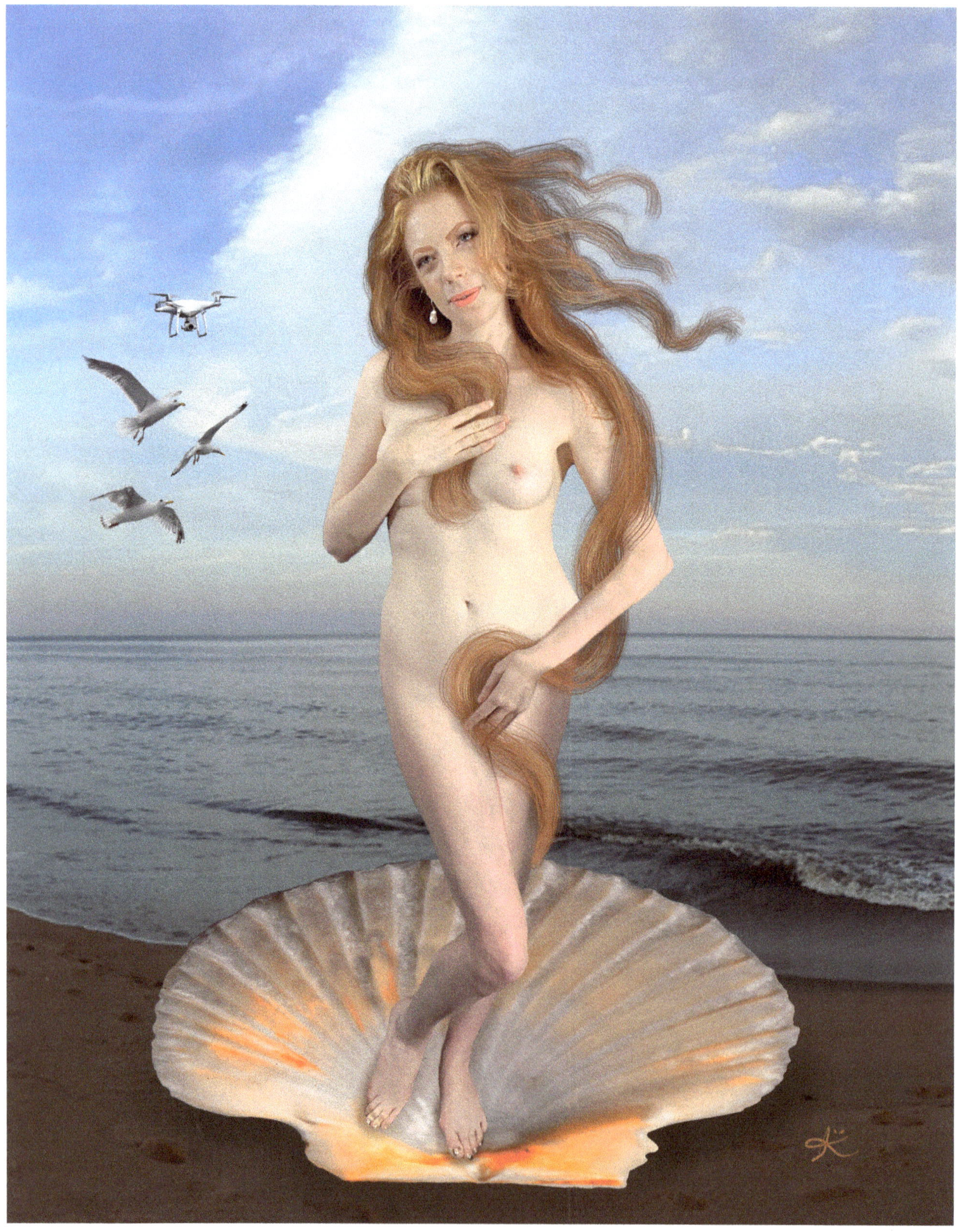

Honoring Botticelli | 2021

HONORIFIC NUDES

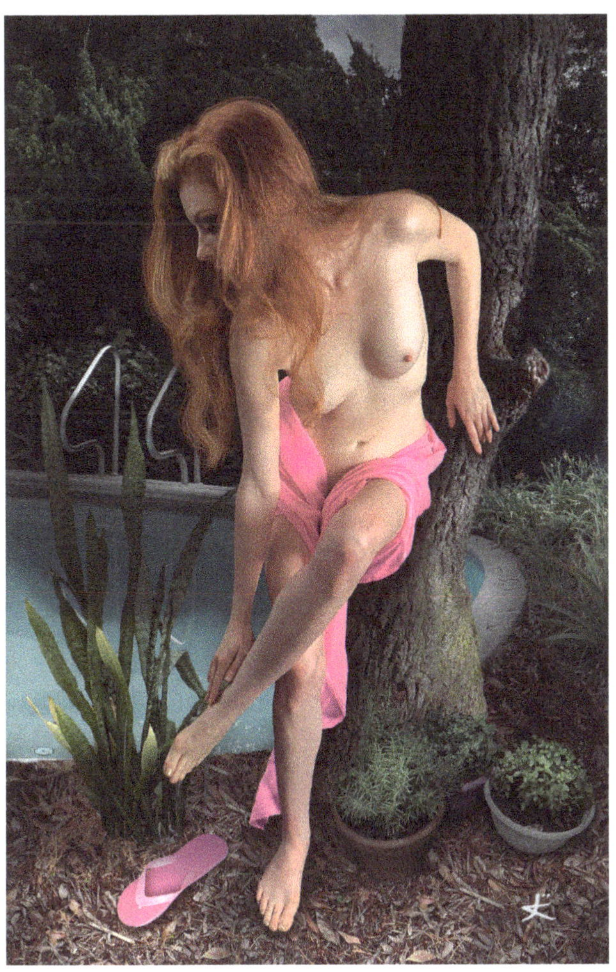

Honoring Da Vinci | 2021

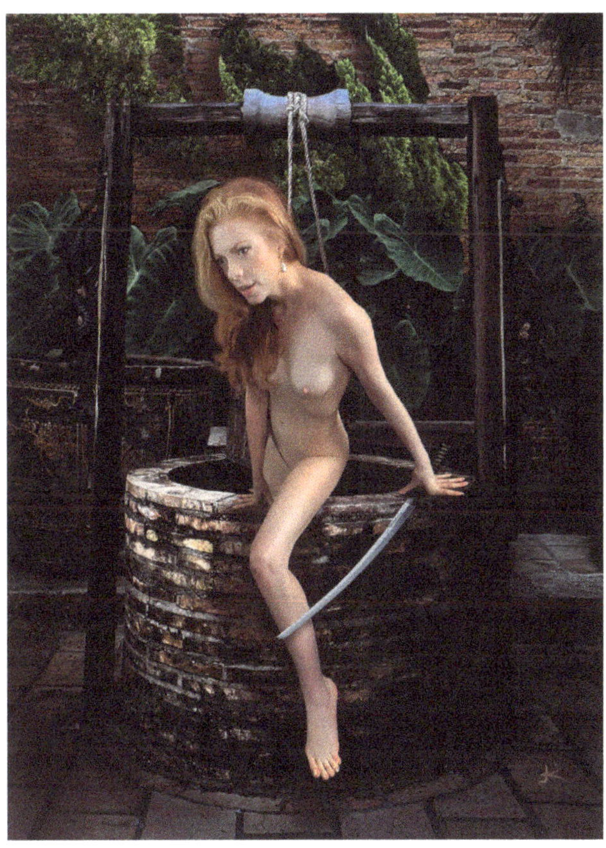

Honoring Gerome | 2021

I had drawn nudes in art class back in college but had never done studies or works of art devoted to the nude form. I was intrigued by the idea of working from a model, especially after seeing some oil paintings by my friend and master artist Mark Miltz. His work, and his nudes in particular, inspired me. Masterful! We both worked from life, him with a brush, me with an iPhone camera and digital brush.

I was not interested in trying to do what Mark does—exquisite brush work using oils, lighting, color, and form done over several months. Yet I wondered what I could do on my own with nudes. I wanted to do something truly unique and worthy of art, and talked with Patty about it. I wanted the series to be classy and artistic.

As I was studying the nudes of past master painters, I decided to create works that honored them and their work, but with a modern flair. I hired a fabulous model recommended by Miltz, set up the studio lights, and we did our best to match the poses of nudes in fifteen paintings I had narrowed it down to. I used my iPhone to capture the images, transferred them to my iPad, and got to work.

We quickly concluded that some of the poses were physically impossible, meaning they were faked by the master painter. What? Actually, I already knew this, but it was fun to sort out how Leonardo and other masters

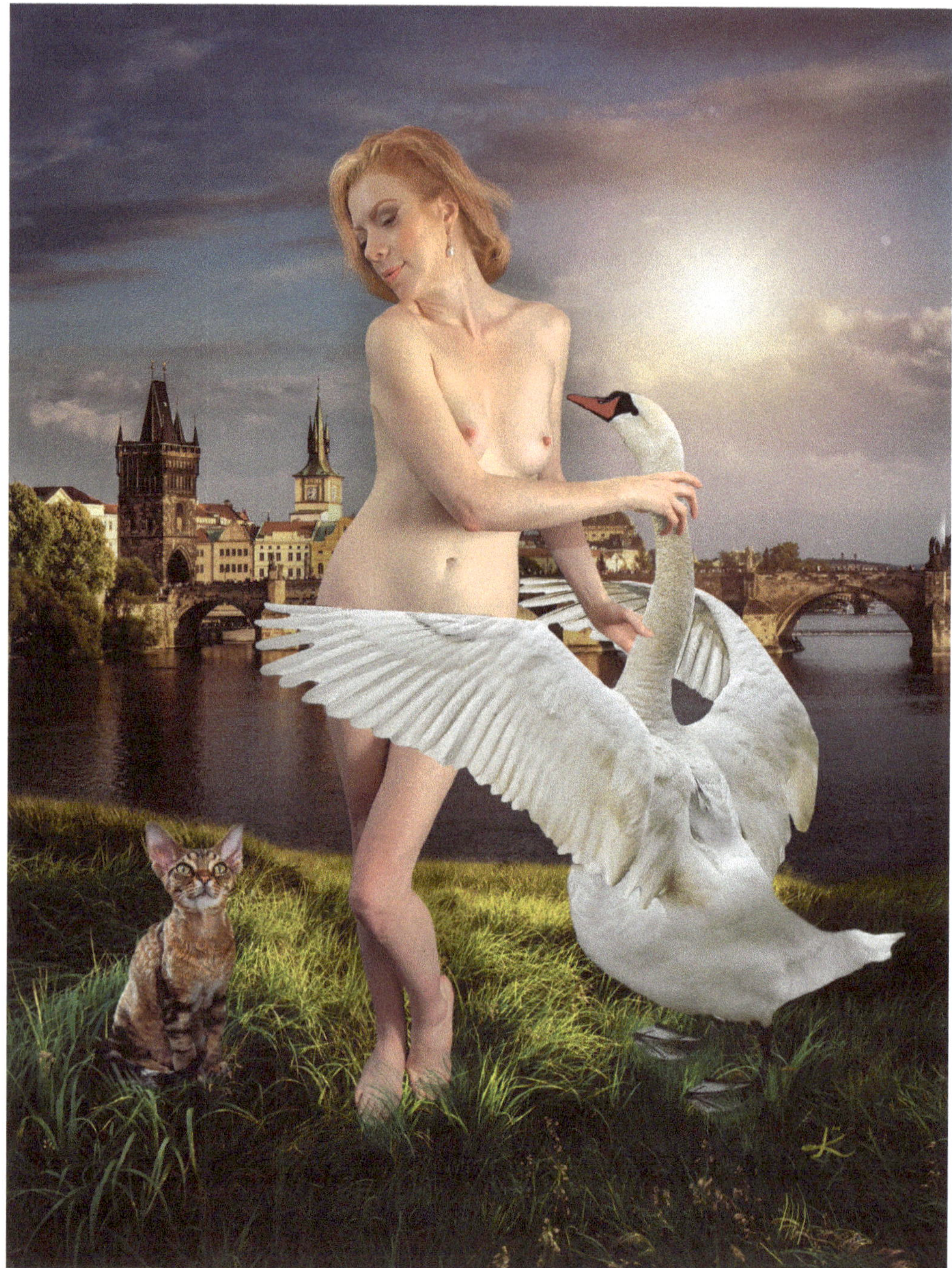

Honoring Da Vinci | 2021

created poses to suit them—not reality.

My technique was primarily photo collage and retouch without noticeable brush work. Each piece required between ten and thirty layers, as I built the background using photographic images of nudes to create a realistic setting. I usually added at least one modern element—replacing a chariot with a car, a seagull with a drone, adding a samurai sword . . . etc.

These pieces took between eight and fifteen hours. I realize that is not a particularly long time for many art projects. But I devoted more time to these pieces than any piece before it. In some ways, it was the culmination of my career as a retouching, photo-illustrator, artist.

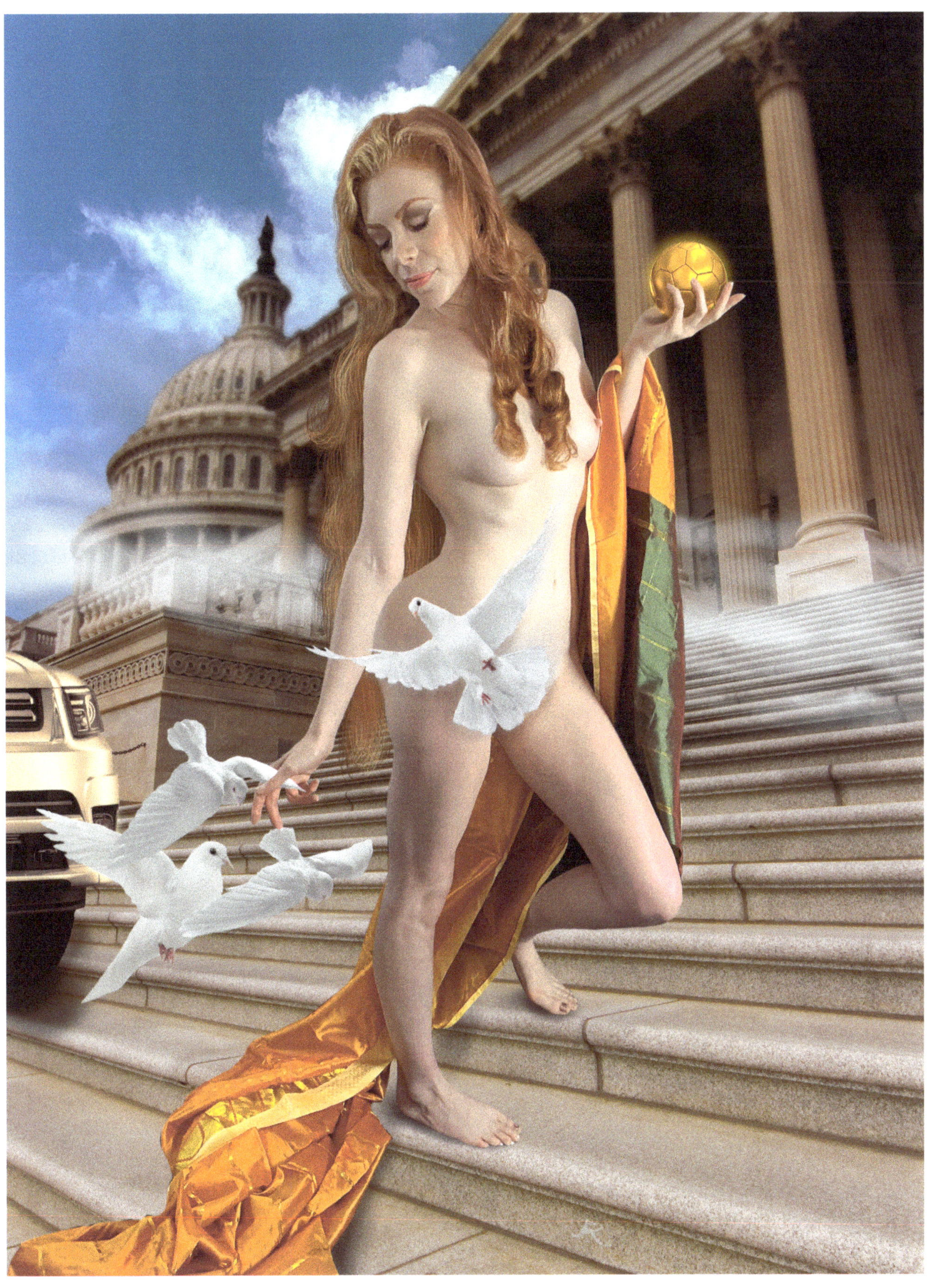

Honoring Cabenel | 2021

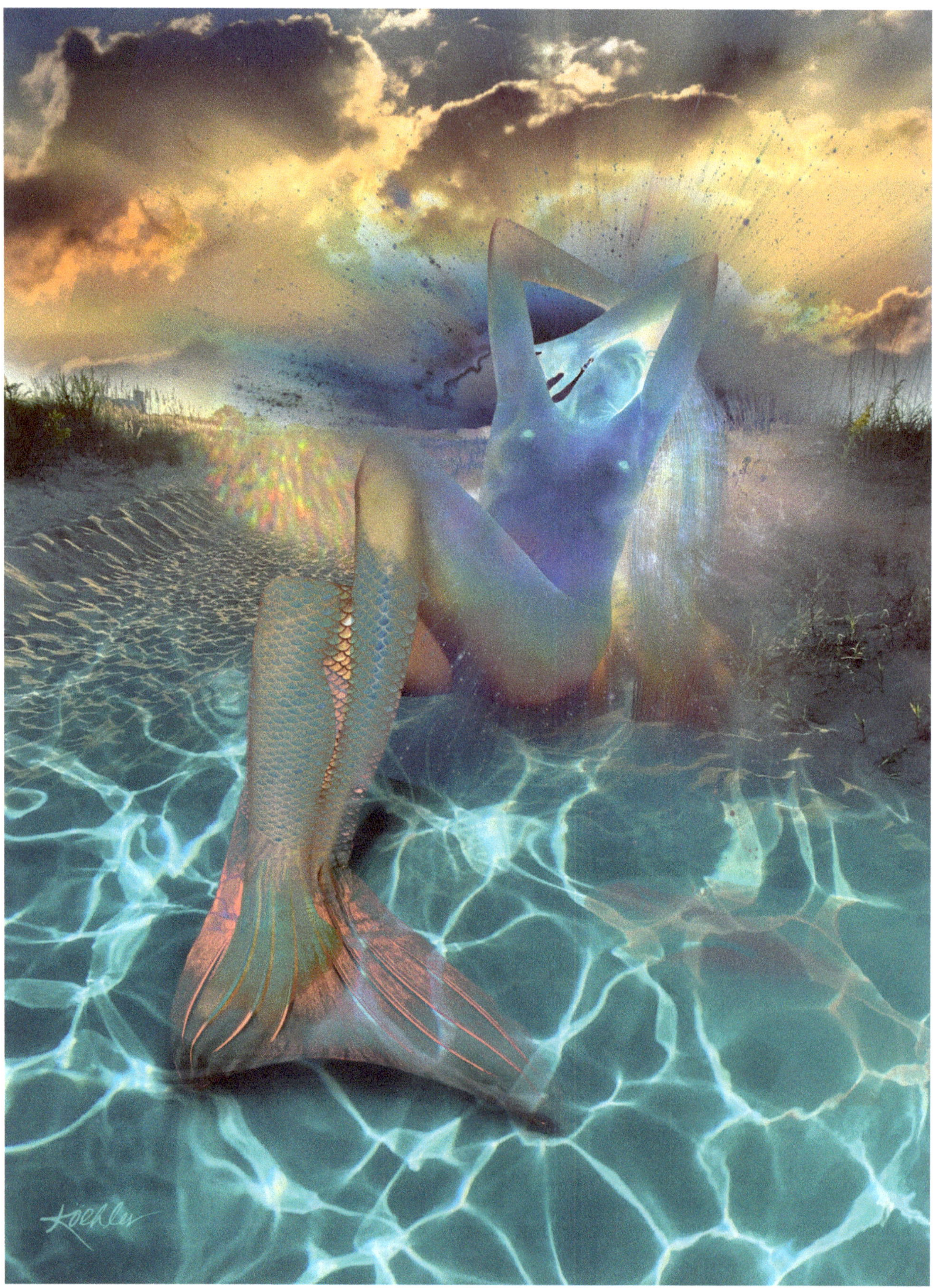

Water Birth | 2022

THE BREAKTHROUGH

In early 2022, I began creating an entirely new "accidental" look. I say accidental only because I did not know exactly what would happen or where I was going. I just knew that I wanted to do something new and different, and get away from the pure representational look I had been using. I wanted to break things down a bit and perhaps abstract them by mixing them together with layers.

I felt quite comfortable with the medium and knew that I had mastered the craft and had the right tools. I no longer had to think so much about how I would go about the process—I just did it. This freed me up to consider other styles and looks.

I took some of the existing nude poses I had and added mermaid elements, since the conventional mermaid wears only a birthday suit. I added the large caudal fin, then several layers of water, sand, sky, dogs, and more. The key was in altering the layers with the use of special effects filters such as "difference," "exclusion," "multiply," and dozens of others to create nonrepresentational looks.

The result was a dreamlike blending of human and natural form that was interesting and fun to look at. The expression and pose of the mermaid became subservient to the other elements, and they blended together to form a whole new look. People could

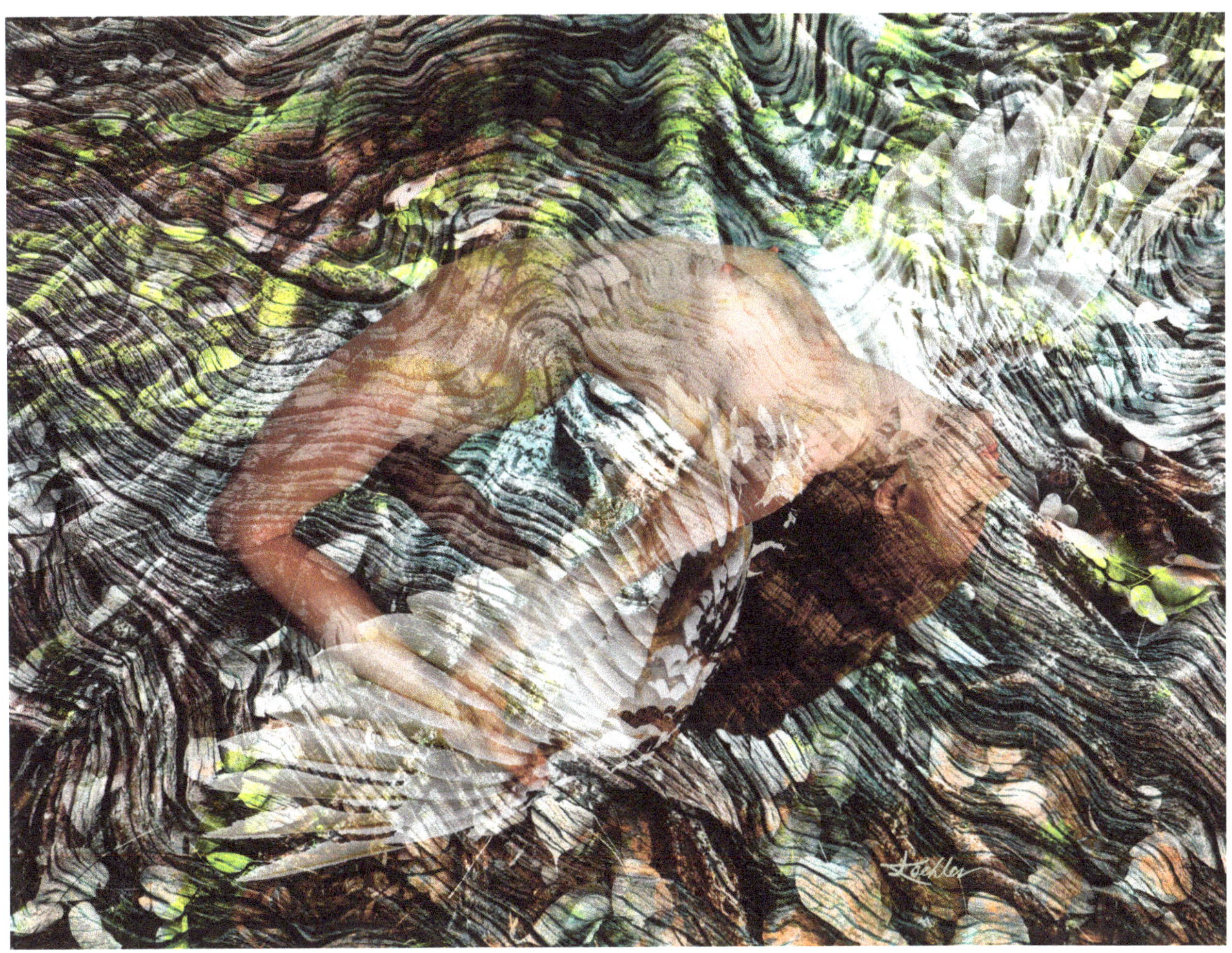

Earth Birth 1 | **2022**

"see into it," and the feedback I got was very positive, including offers to buy the work.

Then I traded the human form for animals and textural photos. Eventually I dropped animals and just used images from nature, whether leaves, woods, clouds, dunes, or water. The effects were quite interesting and the abstractions more than expected. The beauty of this new process is the rapidity of trying out new looks, blending, and colorizations.

I believe that this new look is the culmination of my work over the past four years. Maybe this was a bit like when Van Gogh jumped from drawings and watercolor to oil and realized he had found the best expression of his heart. Or when Michaelangelo had to do clay work before he could tackle marble. They call it art WORK because work is required, along with talent. All artists must deal with this, whether in writing, visual arts, sculpture, music, or dance. You have to put in the time to master your art. I did that in sports with boomerangs, and in business, so why not art?

Hopefully the time comes when you no longer have to think about what you are doing, the methods or tools, and simply do it all naturally. That is the point at which you master your work, and for an artist, it is an amazing moment to achieve.

The biggest change from my earlier work was jumping from representational to abstract. Take, for instance, *Dreams of the Mother*, in comparison to *Sleeping Angel*. *Dreams of the Mother* is surrealistic— yet done in a very representational manner. The most interesting aspect was choosing to remove her body in such a way that it appears the tree branches are her legs. I also did a little shifting of the background texture colors.

Sleeping Angel, on the other hand, is highly abstracted, utilizing multiple layers and varying degrees of coloration and transparency through filters. It also started with a figure and natural elements, but the way they were combined created a much more impressionistic work of art.

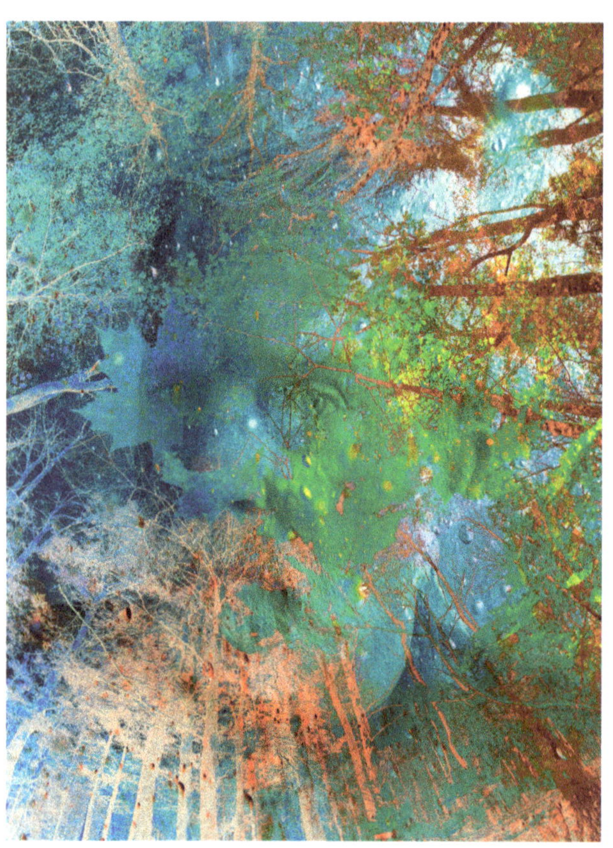

Self-Portrait Layered #1 | 2022

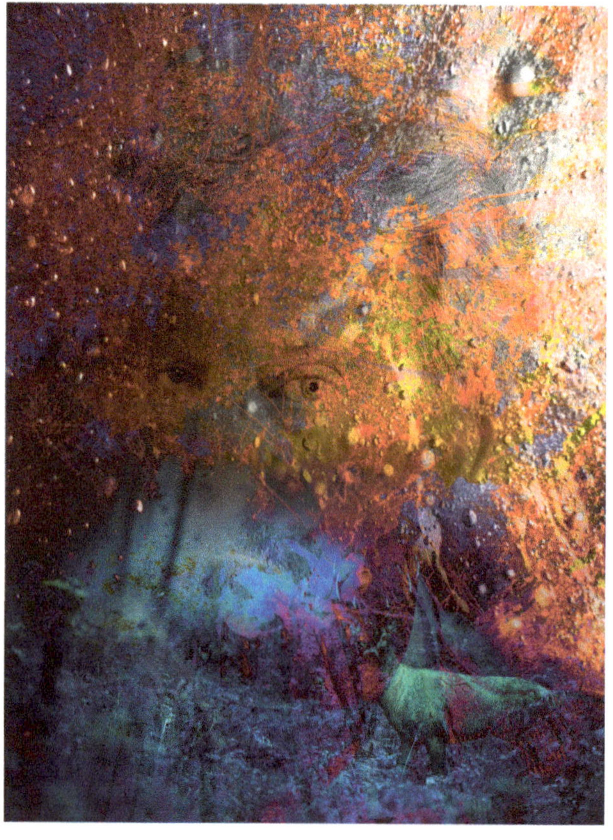

Self-Portrait Layered #2 | 2022

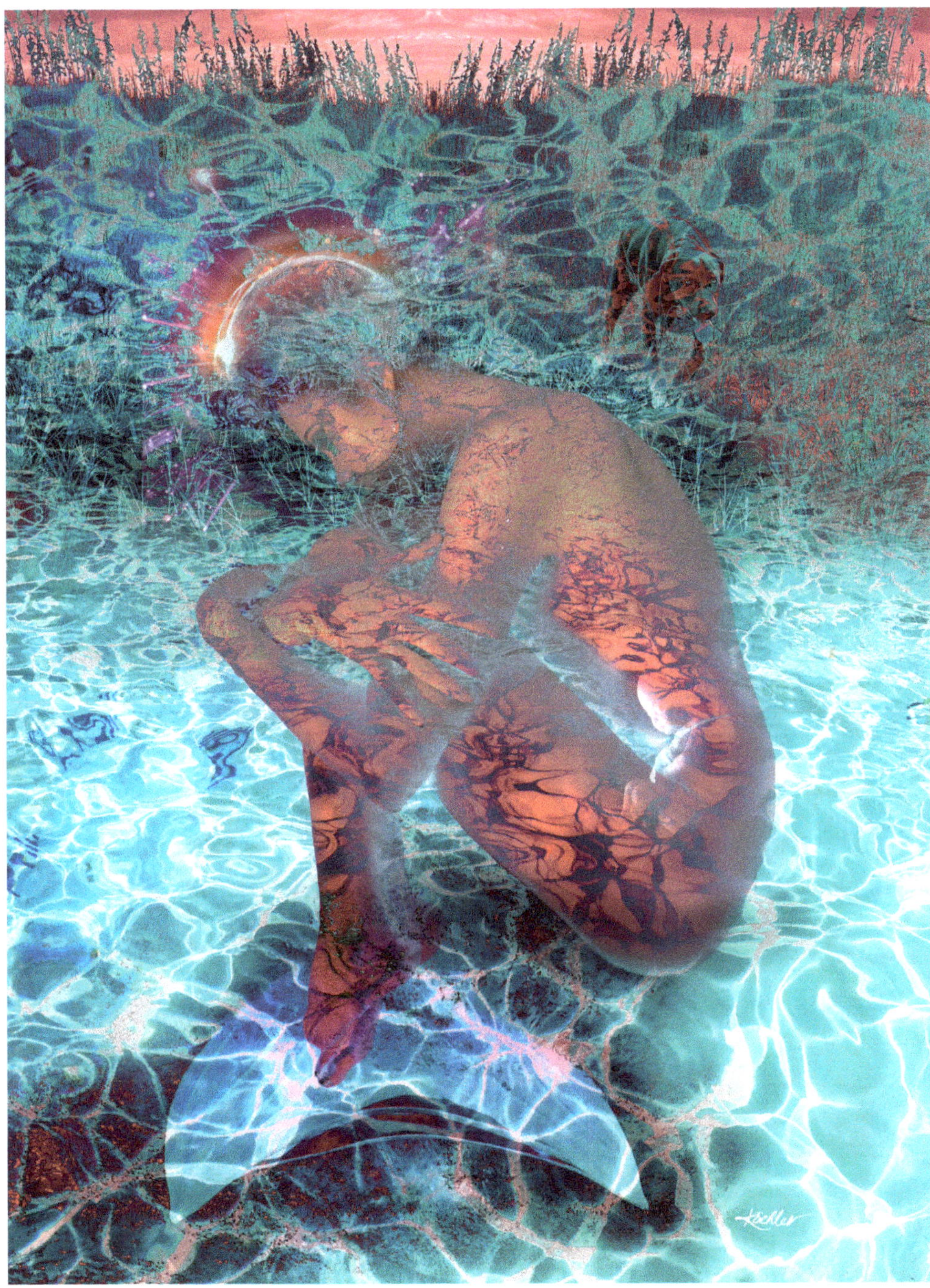

Double Water Birth | 2022

Perhaps the photorealistic and representational works were the necessary ways for me to discover this new way. I'm not suggesting it is my final look at all—just saying that it was wonderful to discover it.

I know from my art history lessons that many abstract painters first learned to draw, paint, and sculpt well from life, and then from that knowledge, they were able to break down that life into abstractions of design and color. Perhaps, during the later stages of my life and art career, this is what I am doing . Perhaps I just got lucky. Or perhaps a bit of both.

Either way, I shall continue my quest to create compelling art that pleases me, and may, in fact, please others. We shall see. But for now . . . bon appétit!

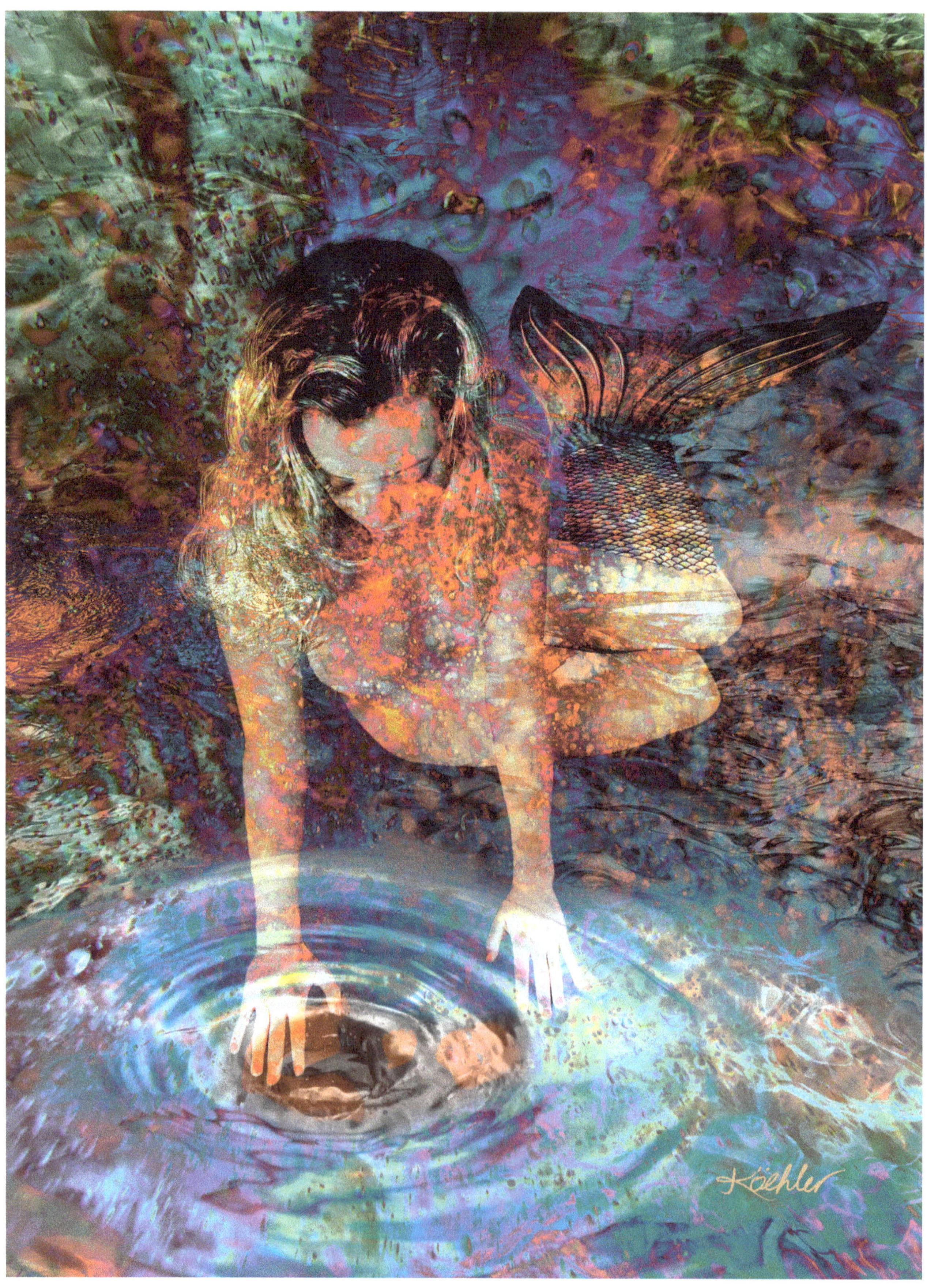

Water Birth 5 | 2022

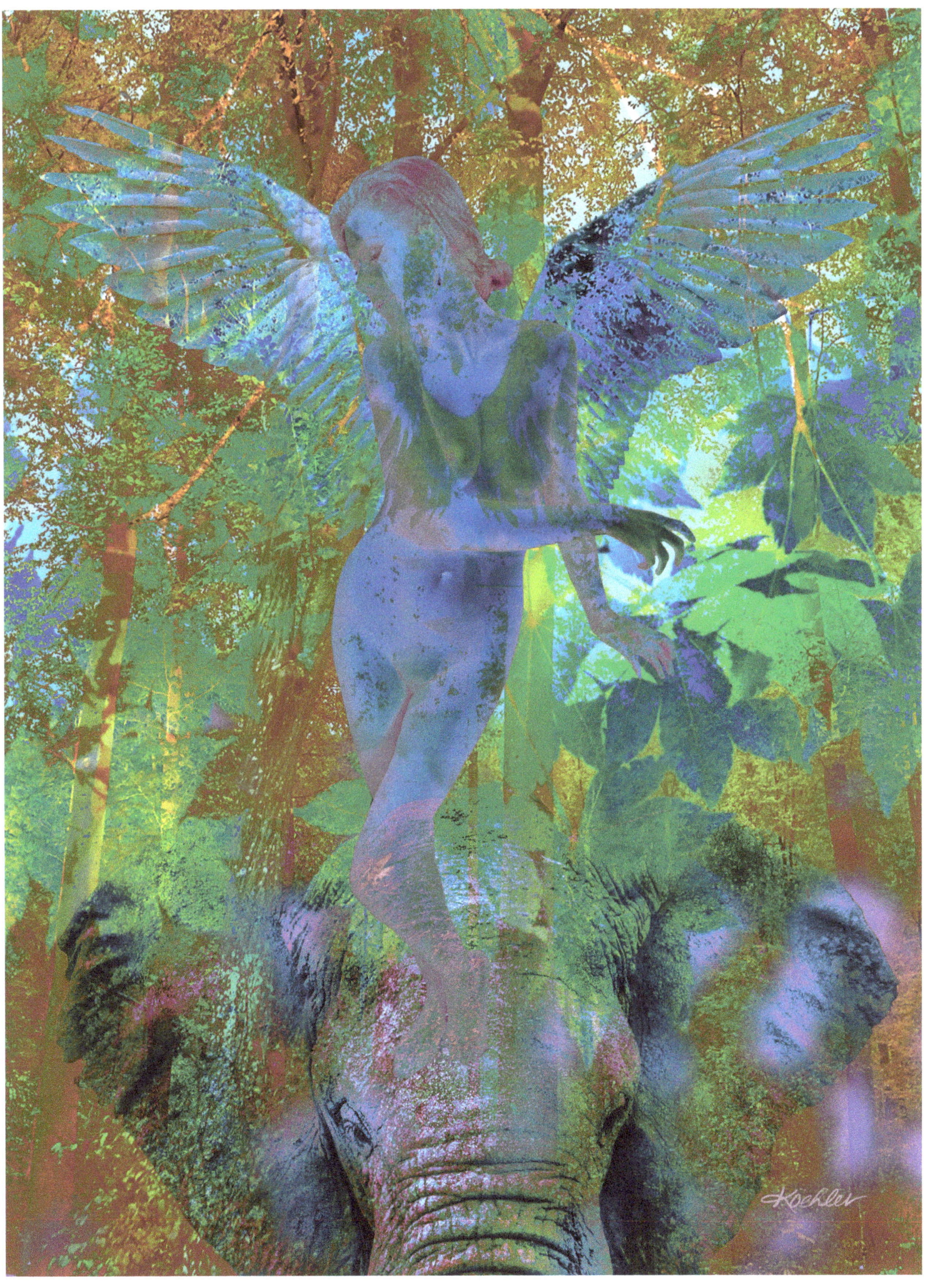

The Arrival | 2022

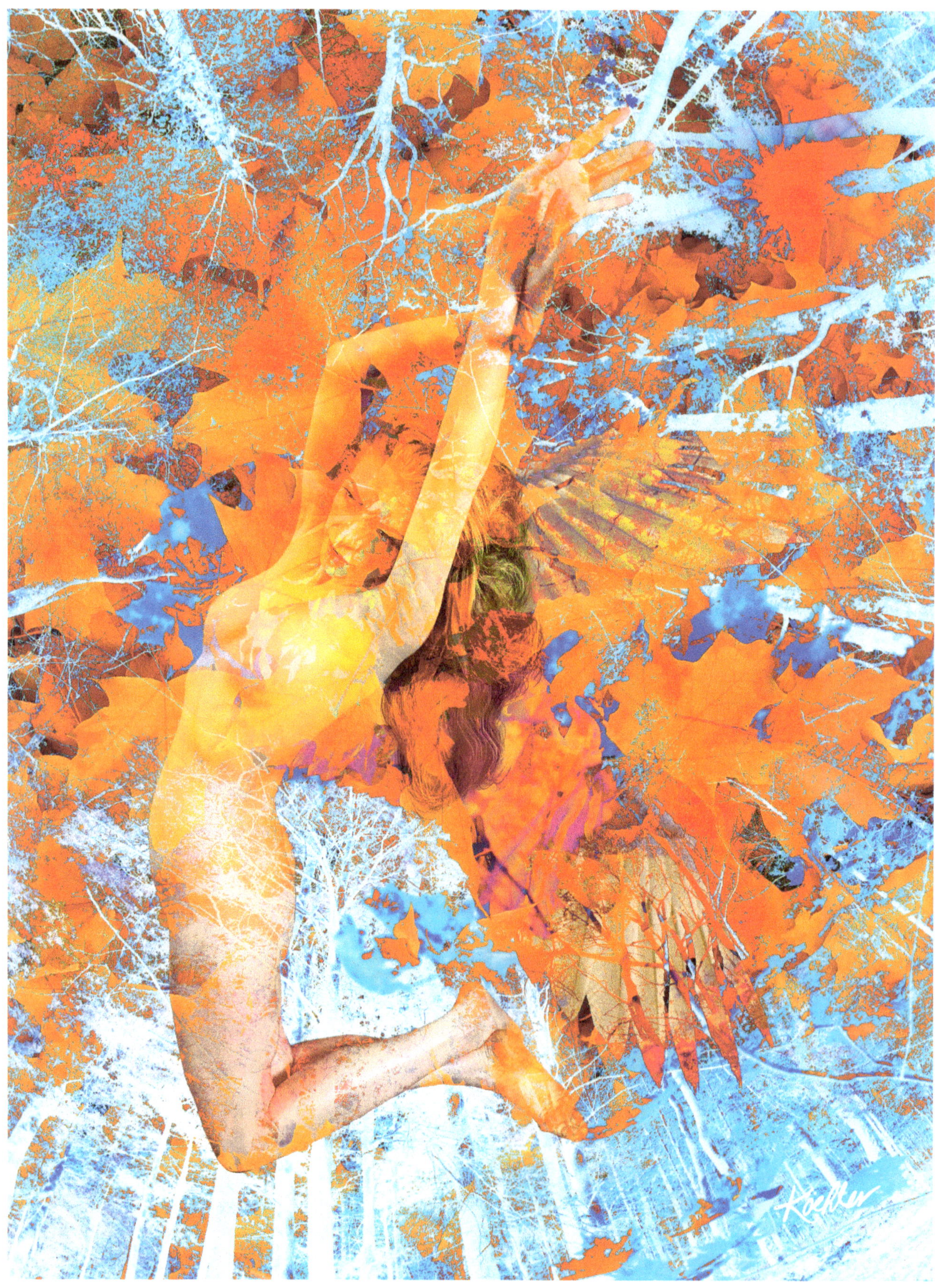

Earth Birth 2 | 2022

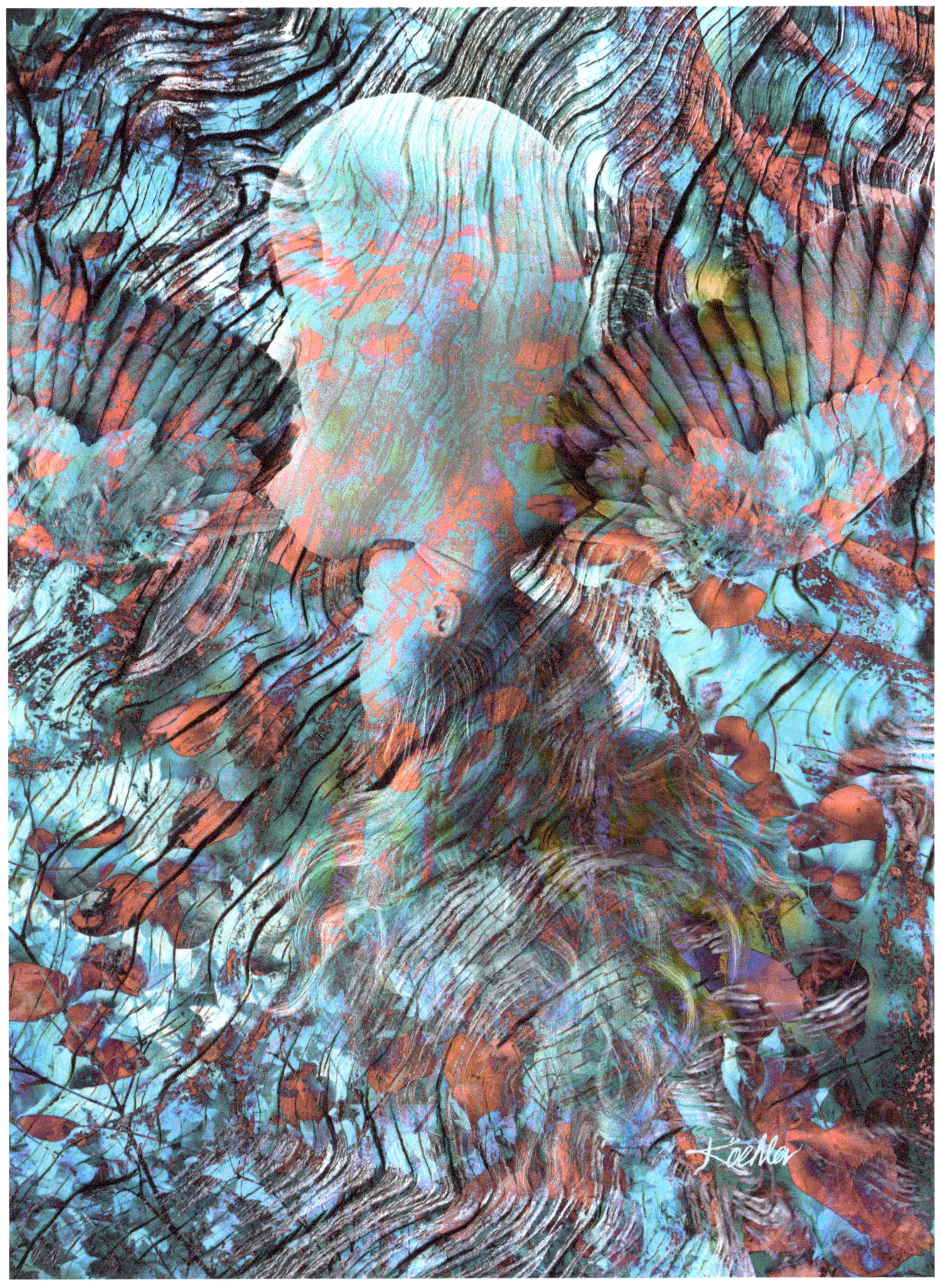

Sleeping Ängel | 2022

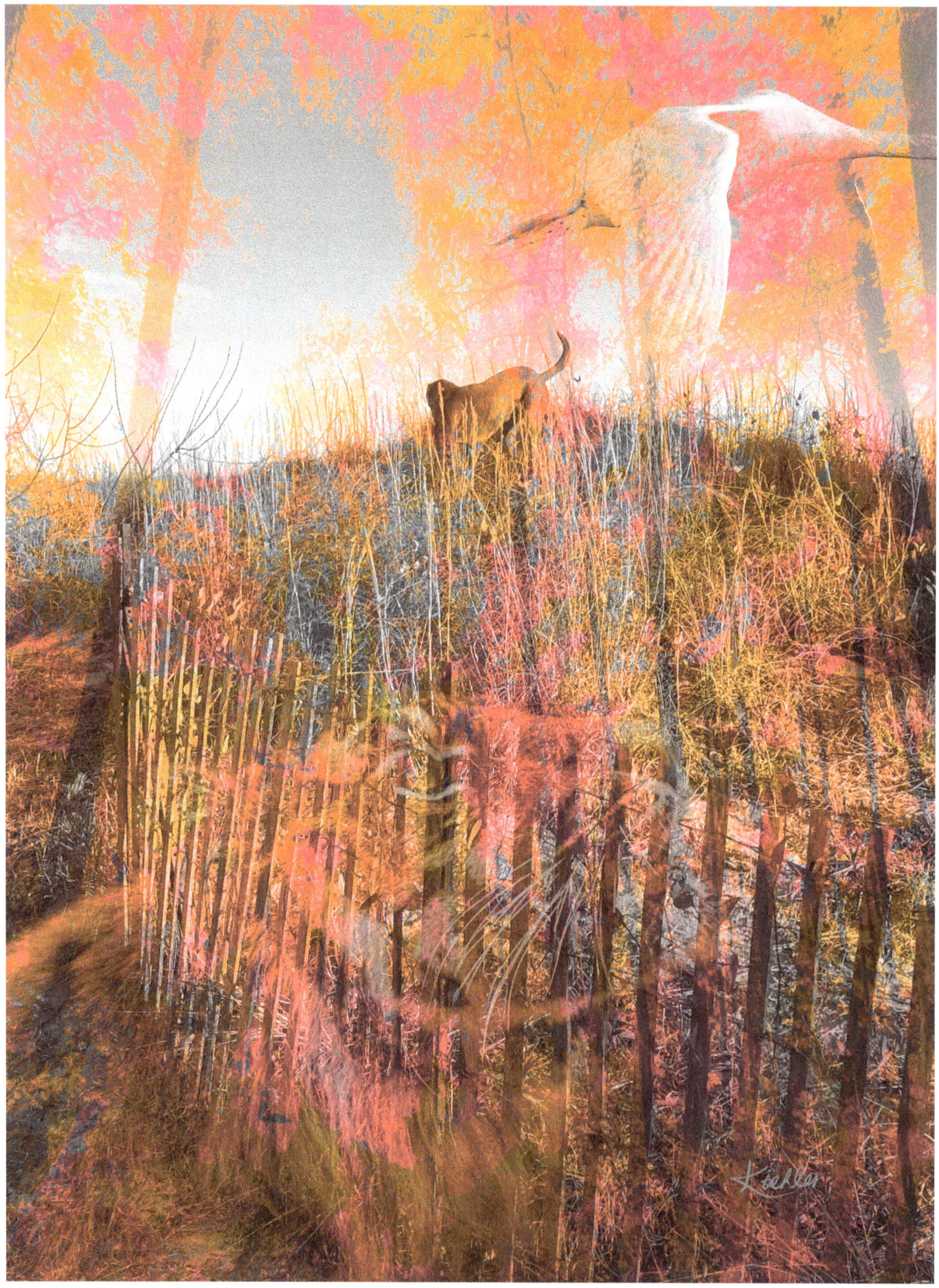

Hidden Tiger | 2022

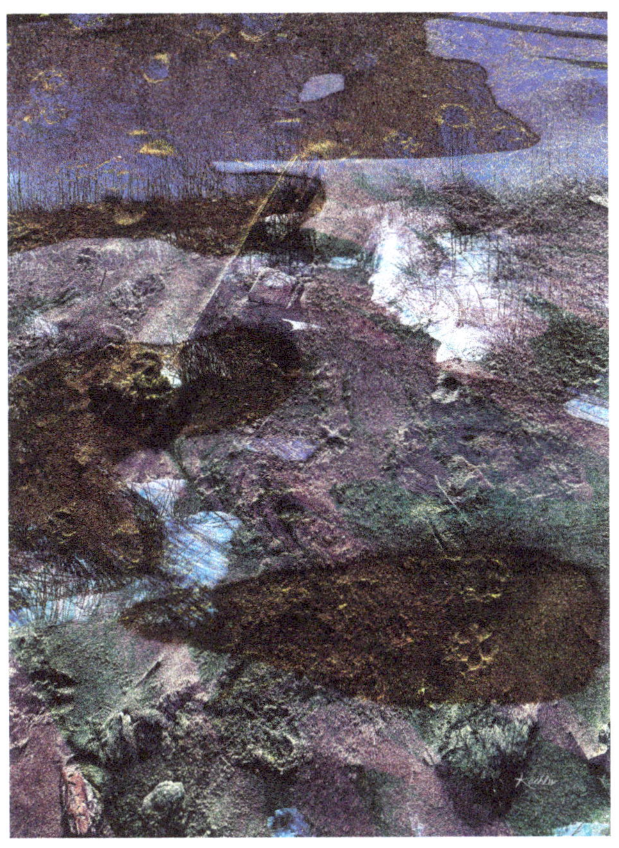

Snow Beach | 2022

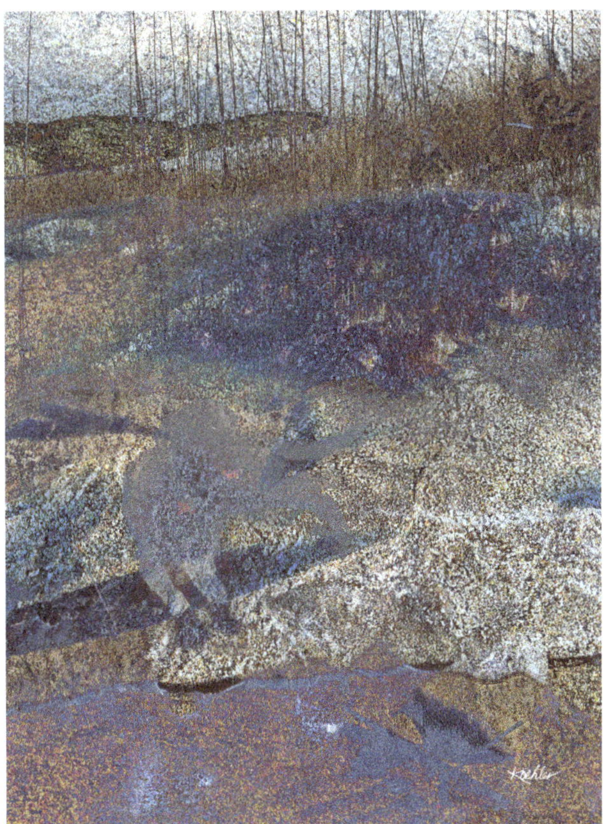

Obliterated Dune Dog | 2022

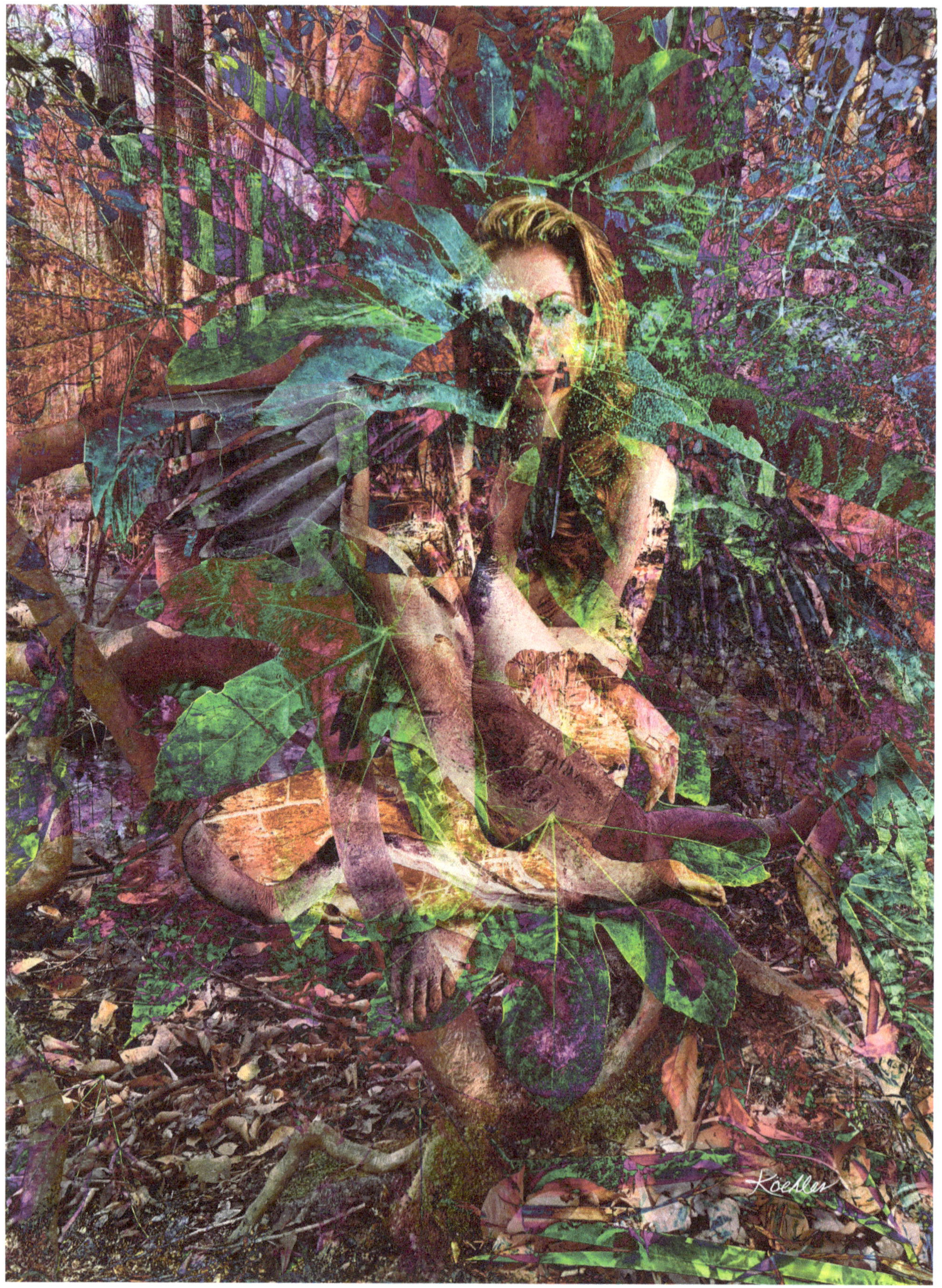

Jungle Angel | 2022

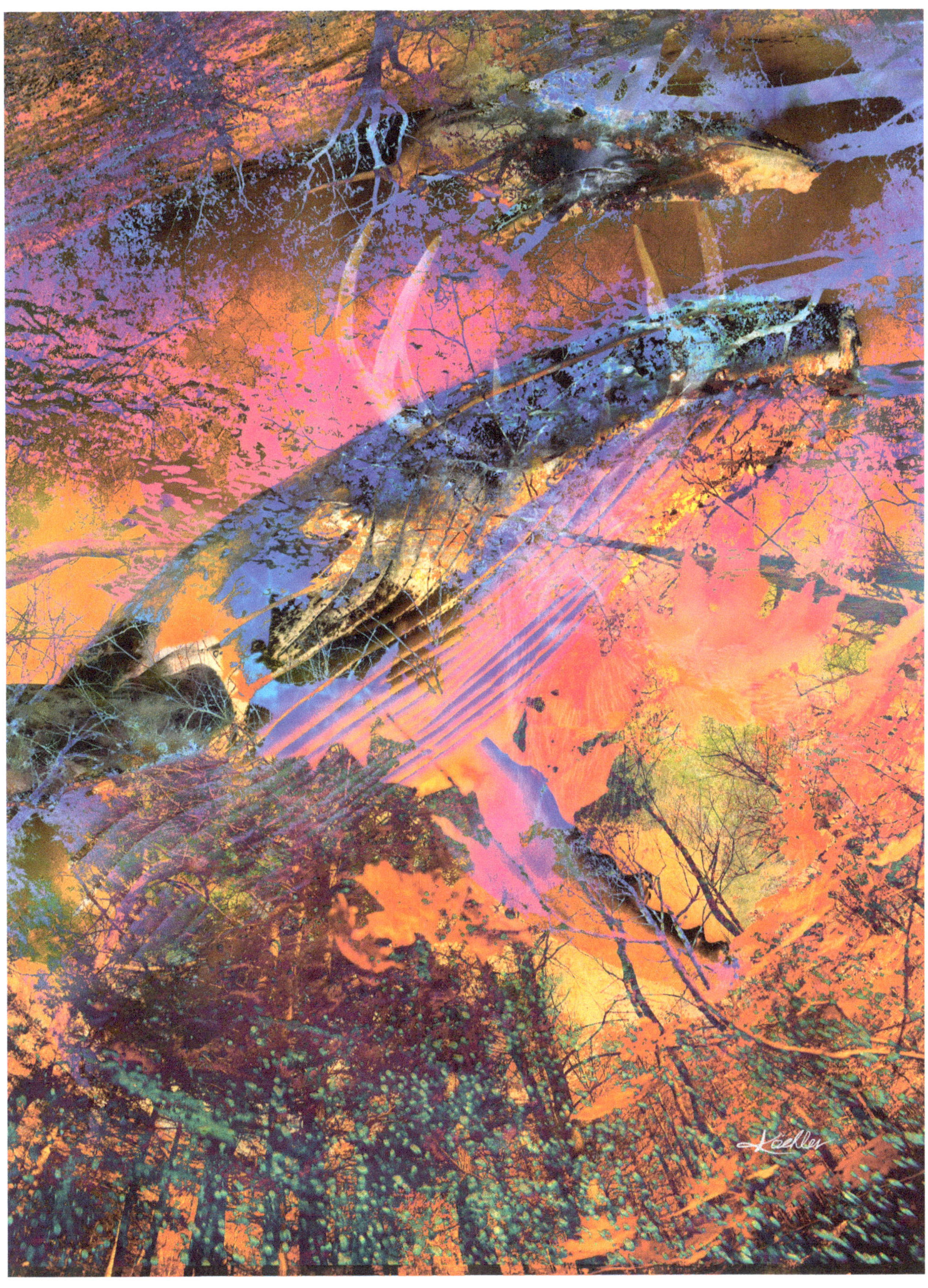

Land & Sea | 2022

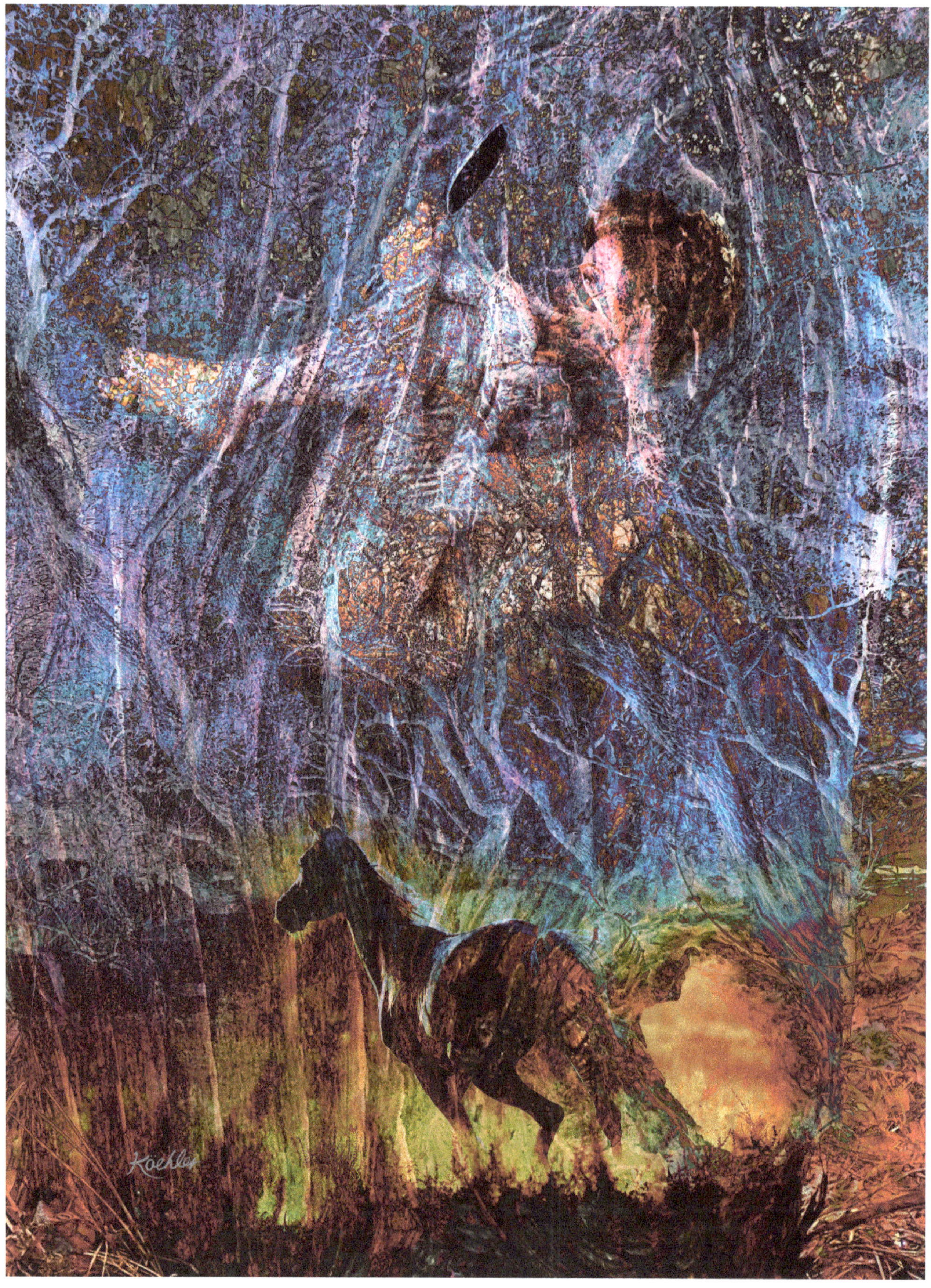

Falling Horse | 2022

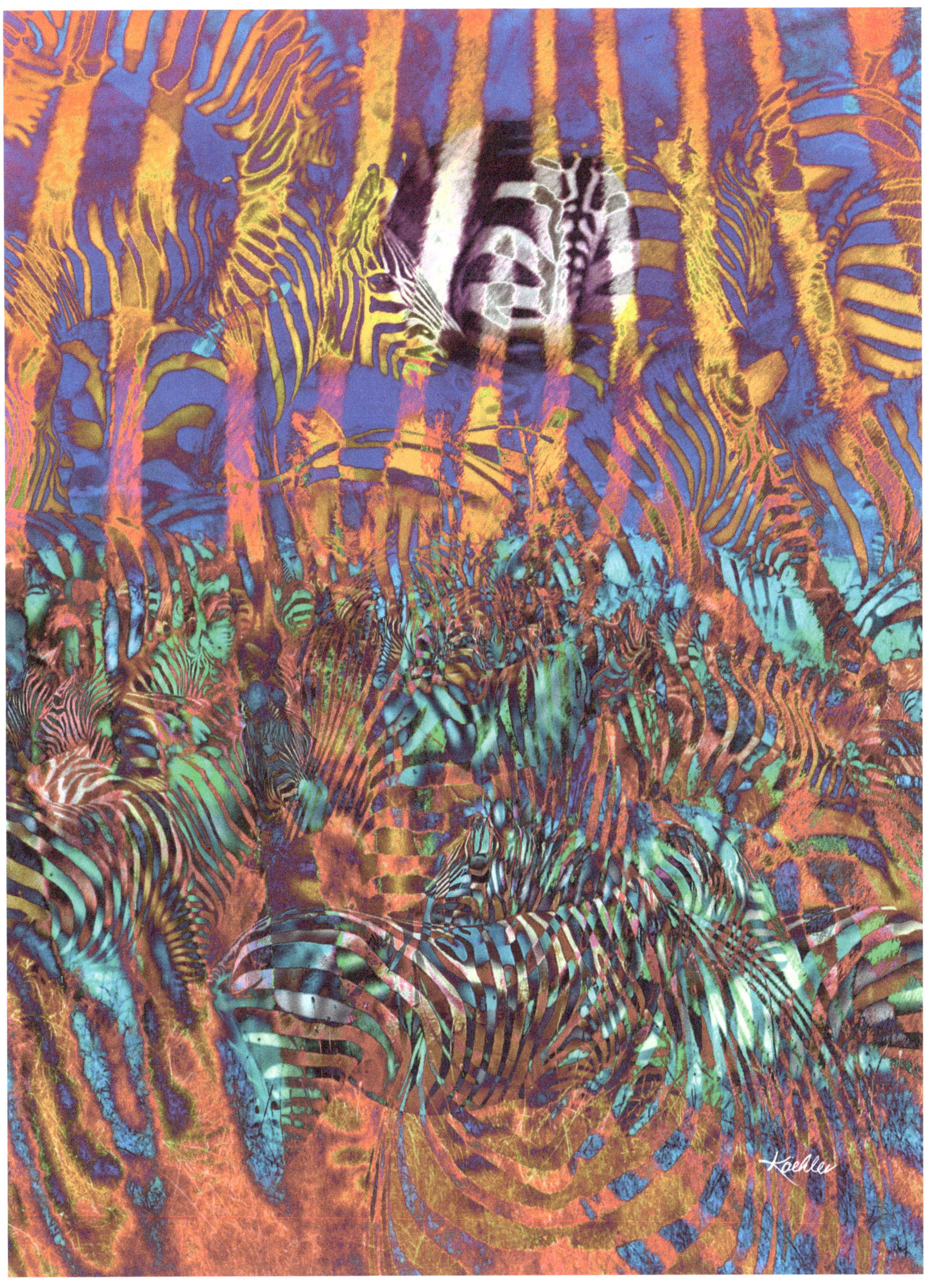

Zebra | 2022

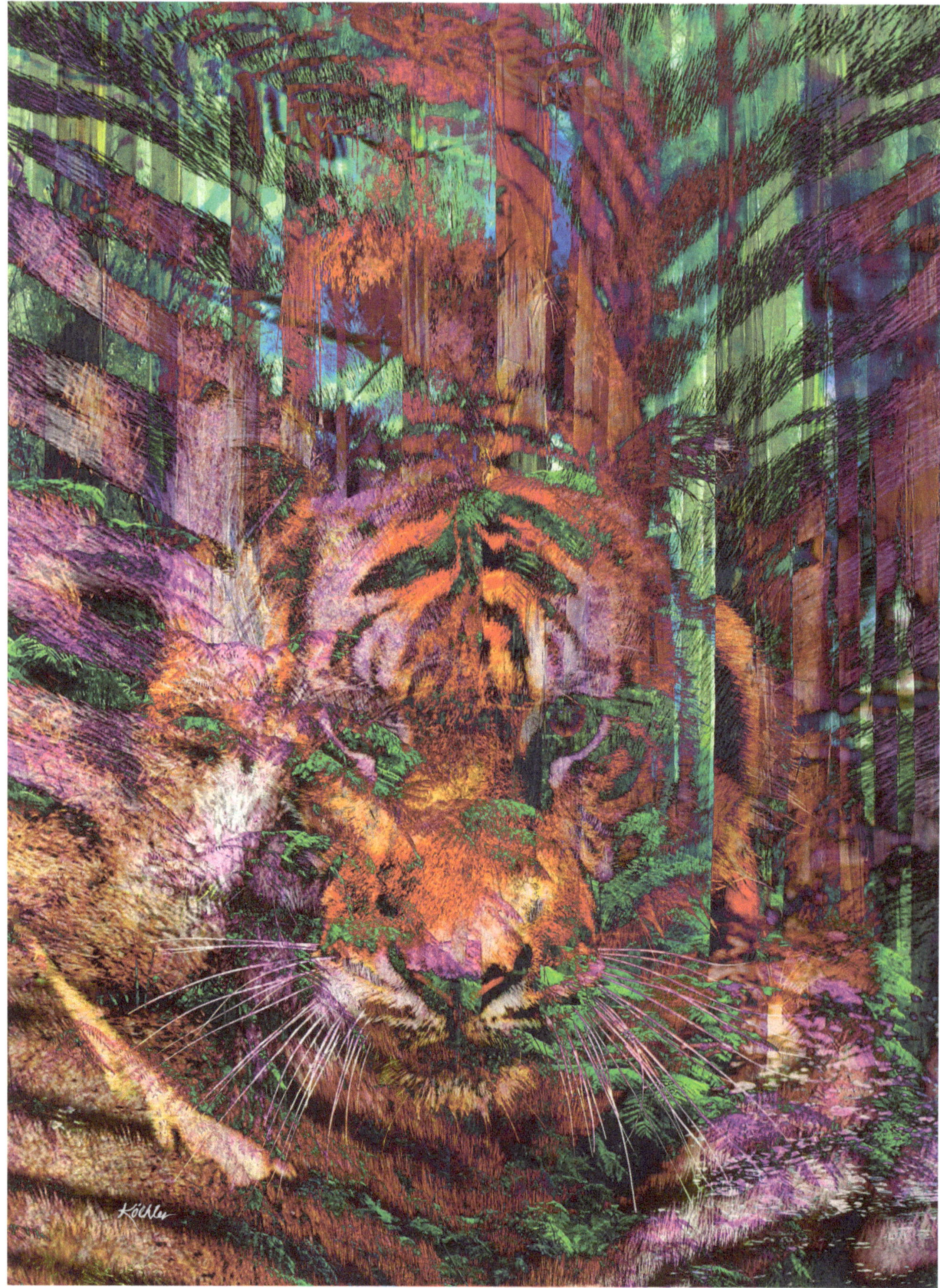

Tiger | 2022

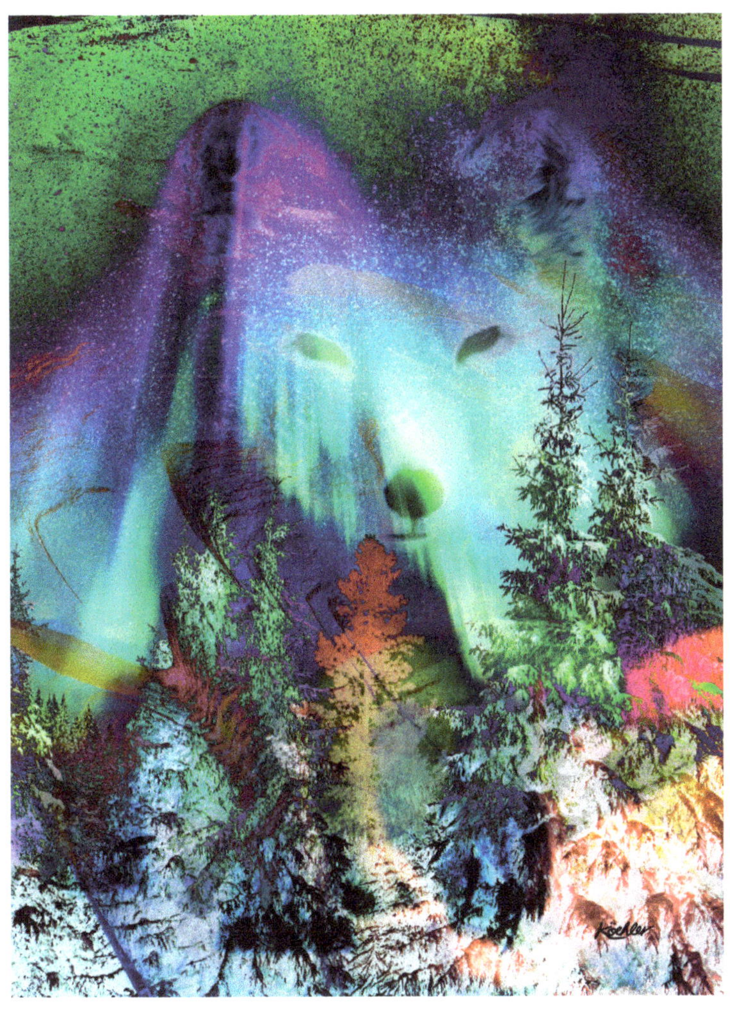

Arctic Fox 1 | **2022**

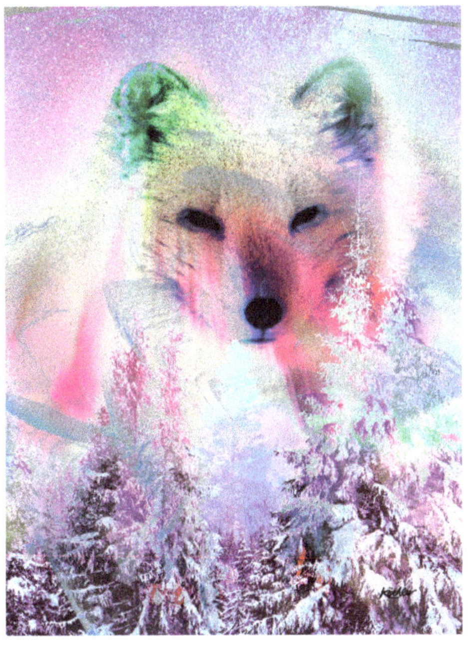

Arctic Fox II | **2022**

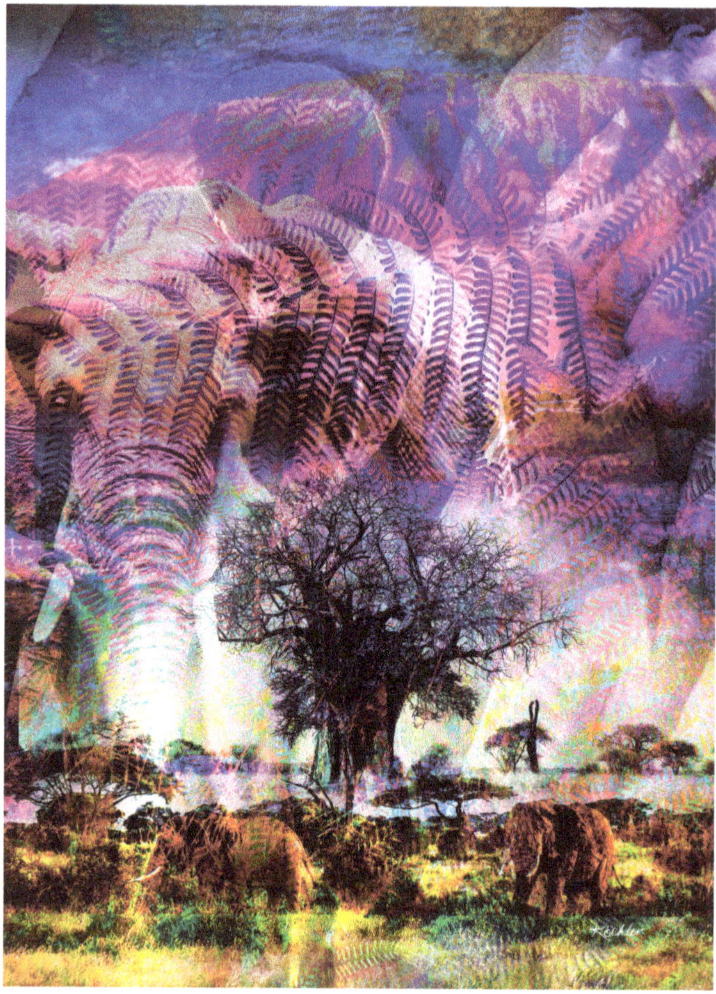

African Elephant | 2022

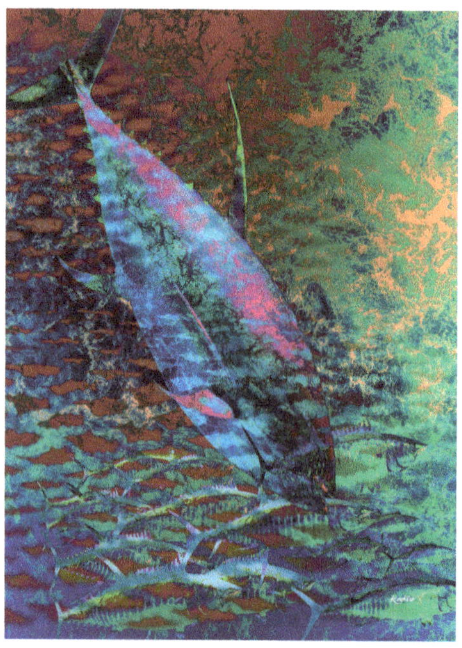

Yellowfin Tuna | 2022

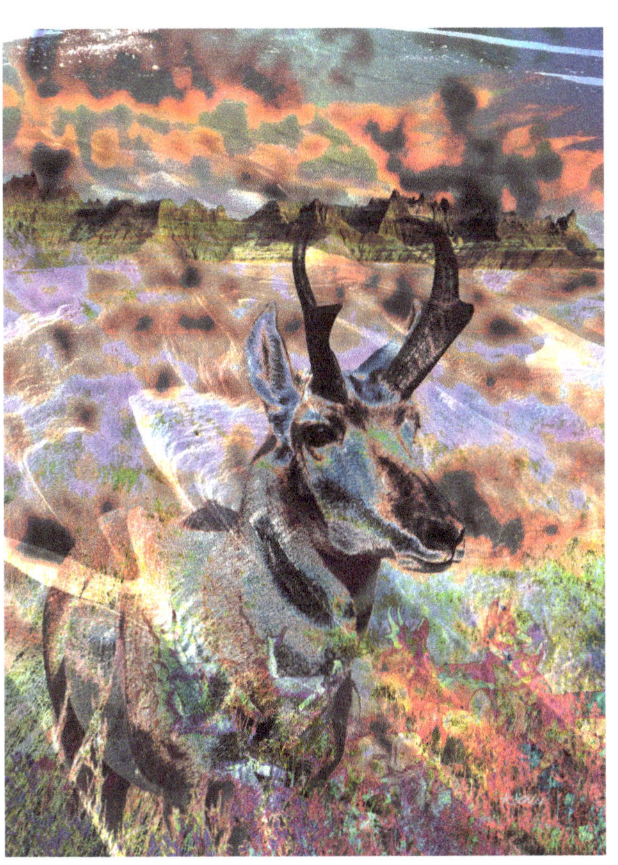

Pronghorn Antelope | 2022

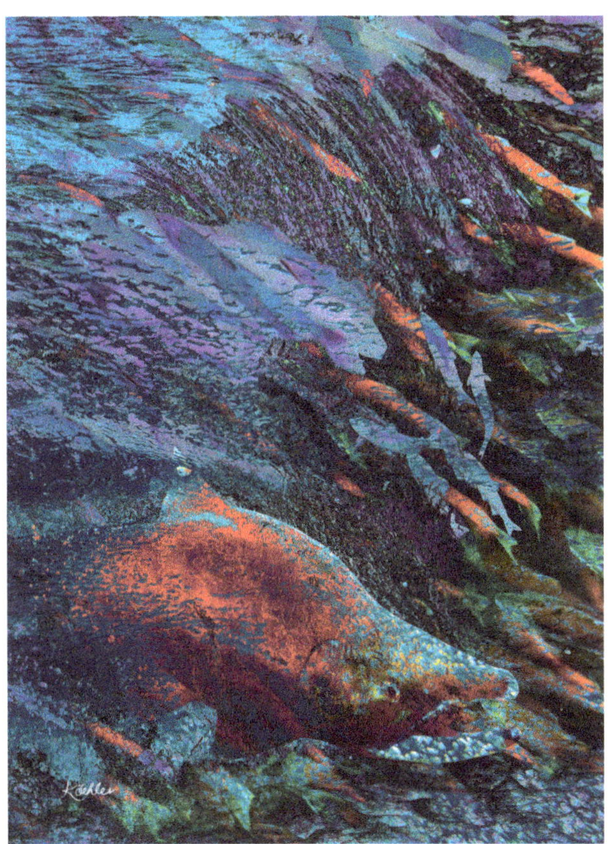

Salmon & Bear | 2022

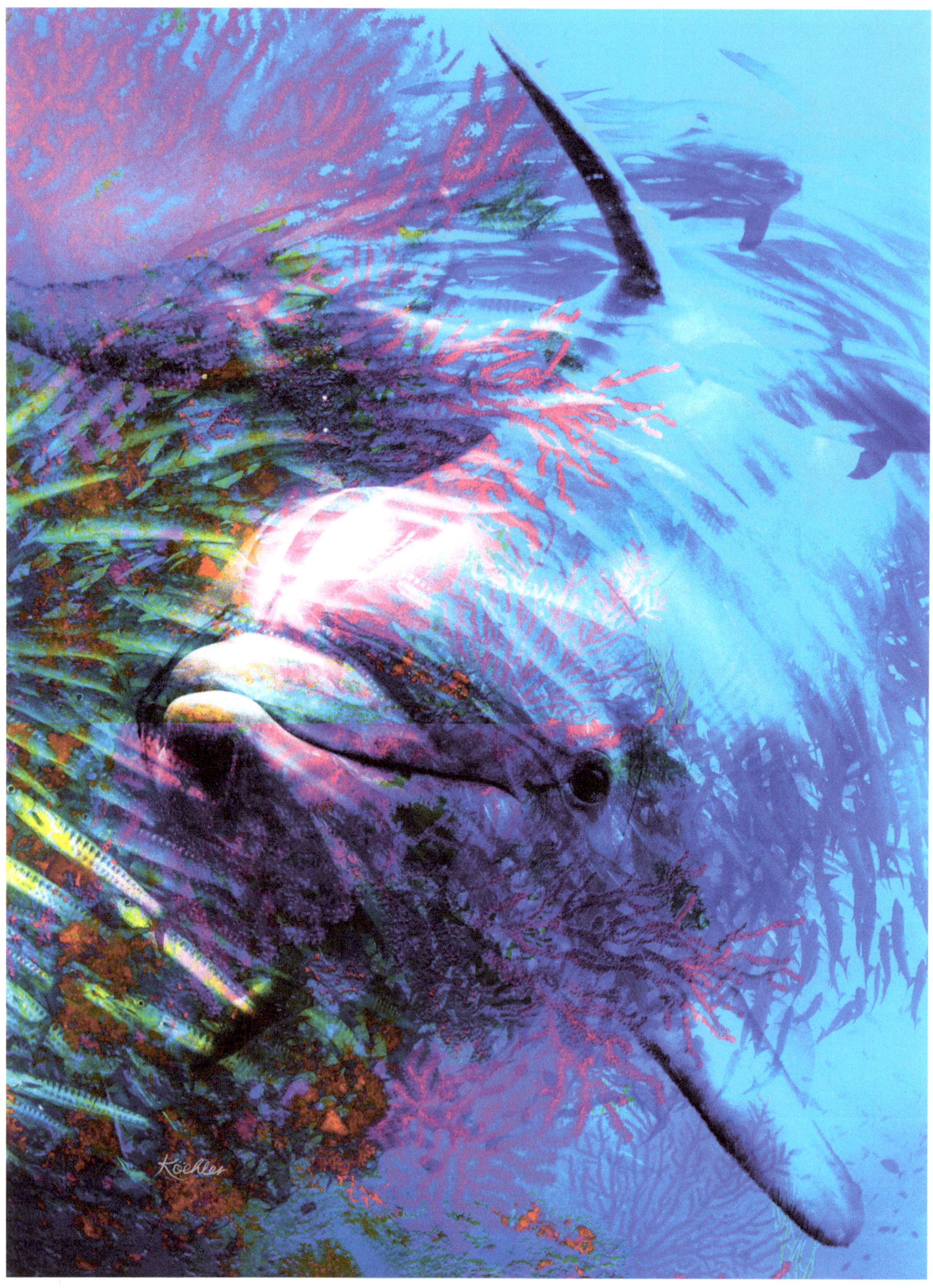

Bottlenose Dolphin | 2022

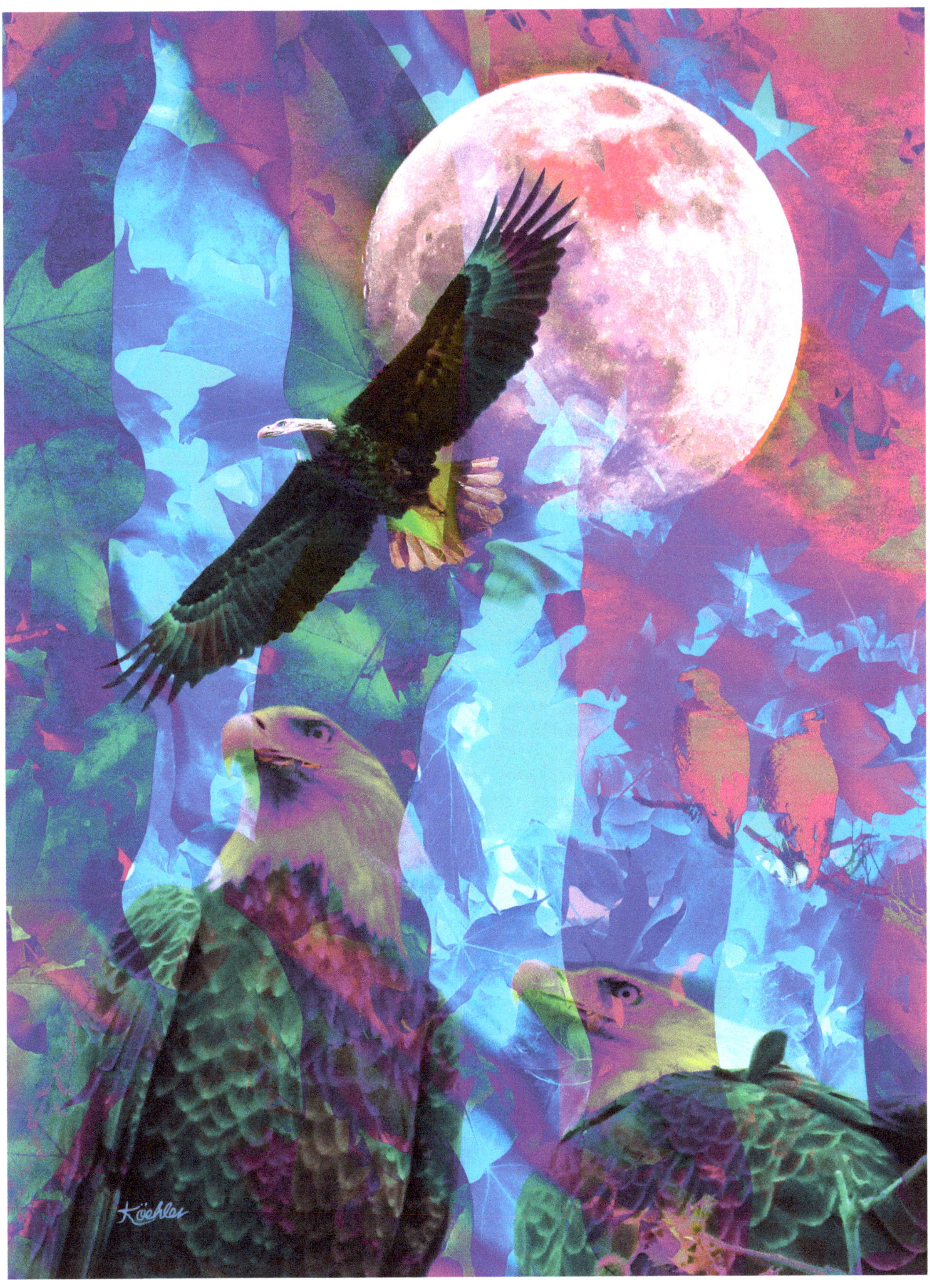

Bald Eagle | 2022 (eagle photos by Chet Snouffer)

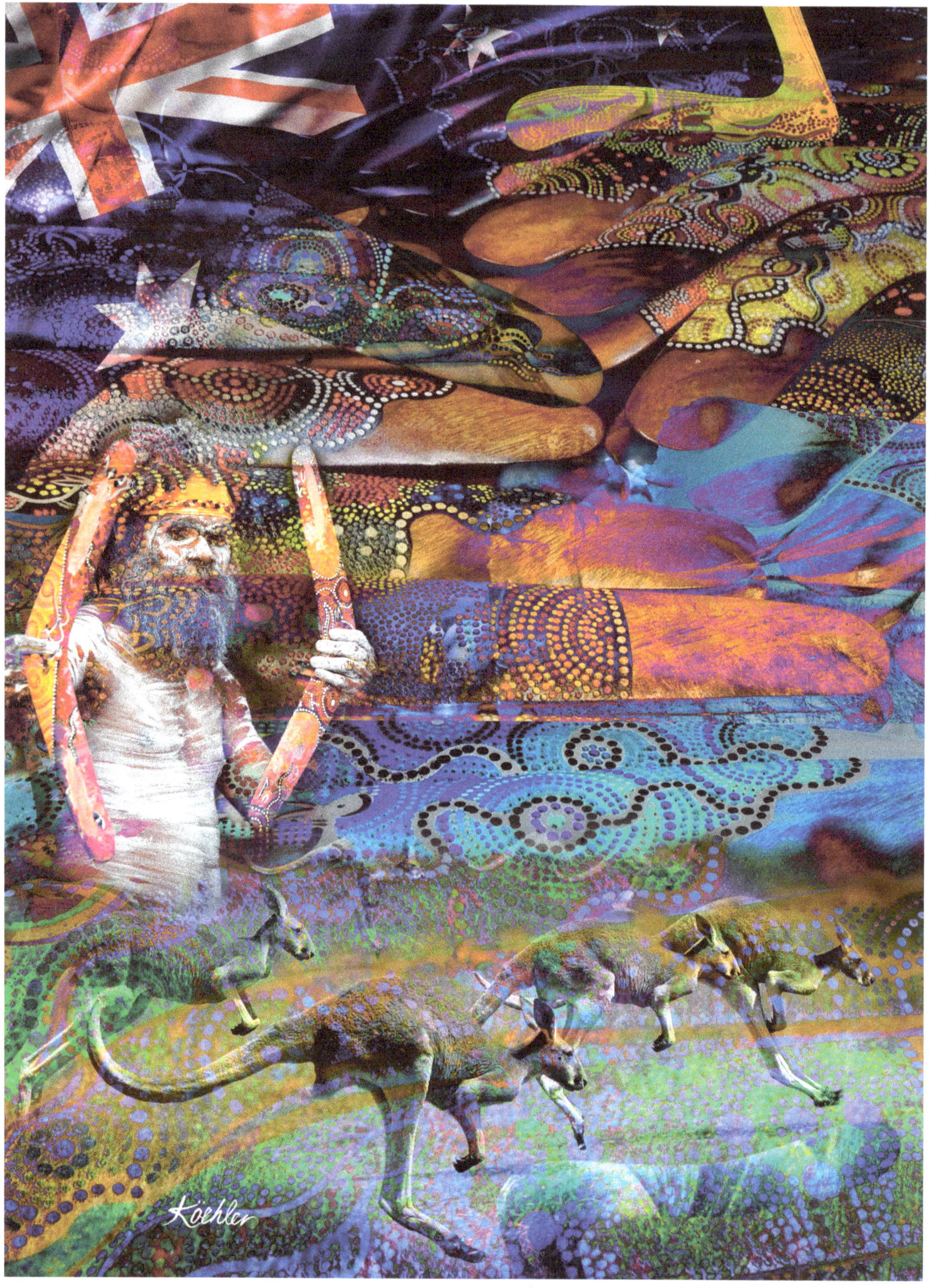

Aussie Boomerangs | 2022

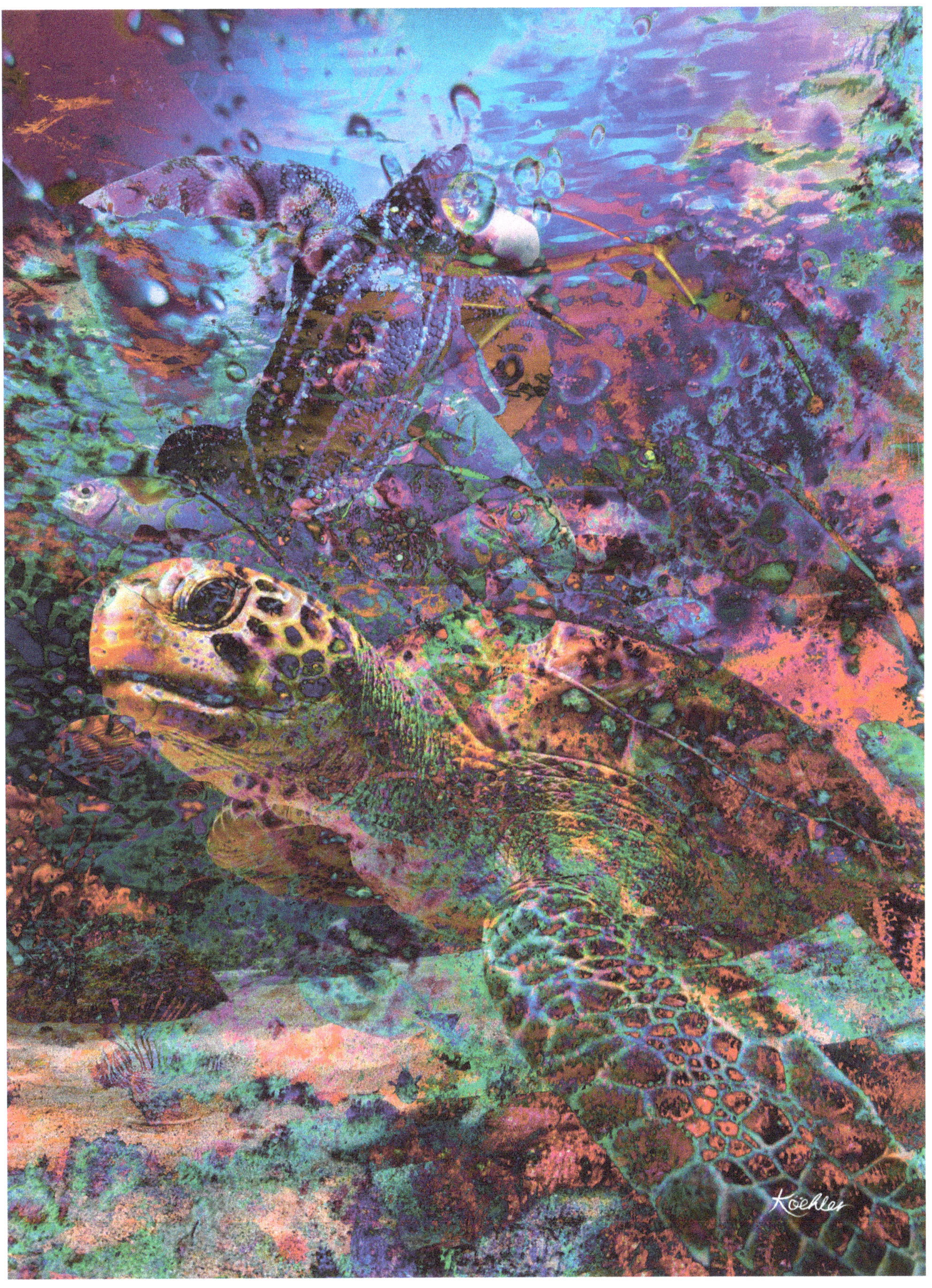

Sea Turtle | 2022

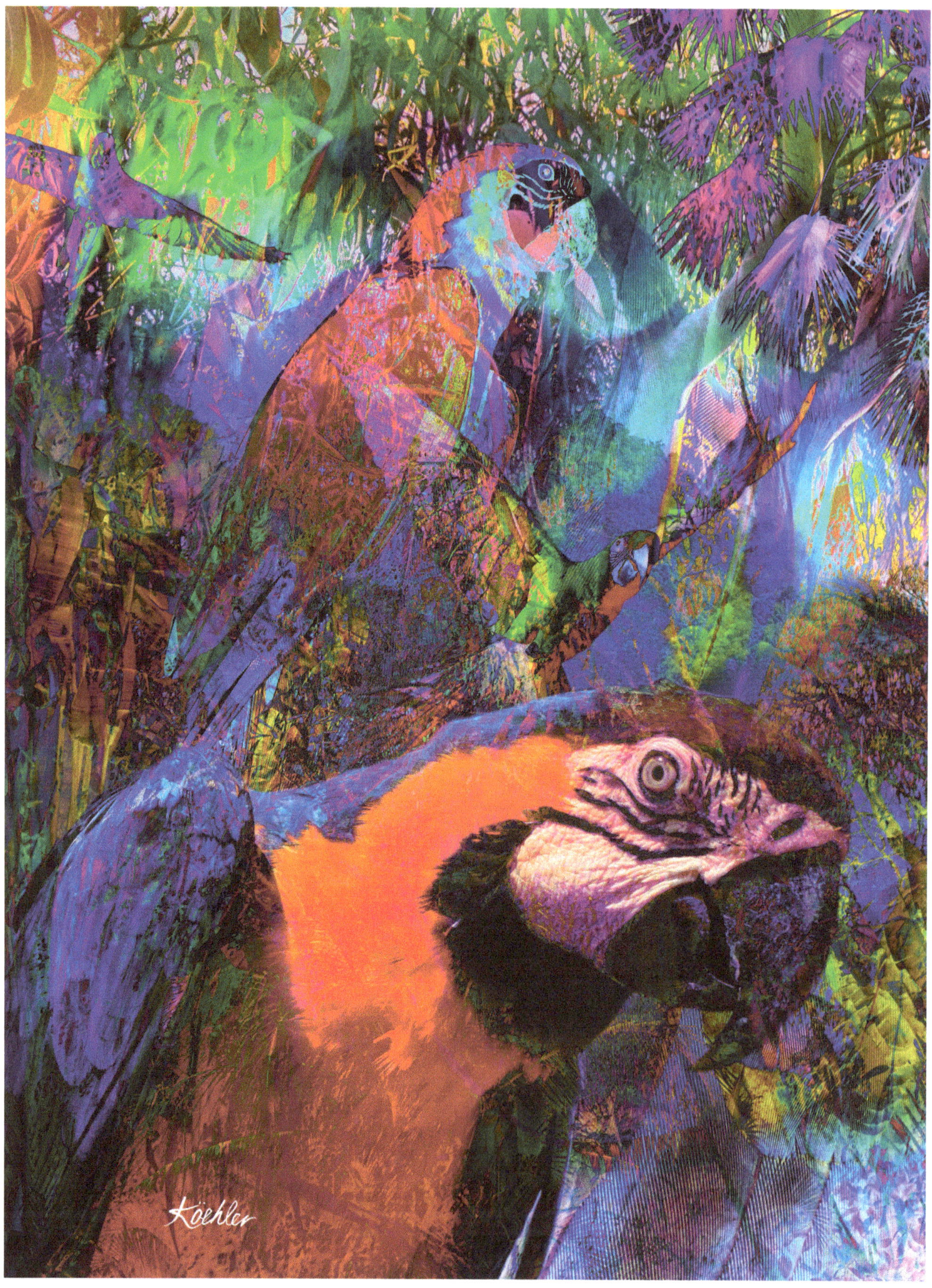

Parrot | 2022

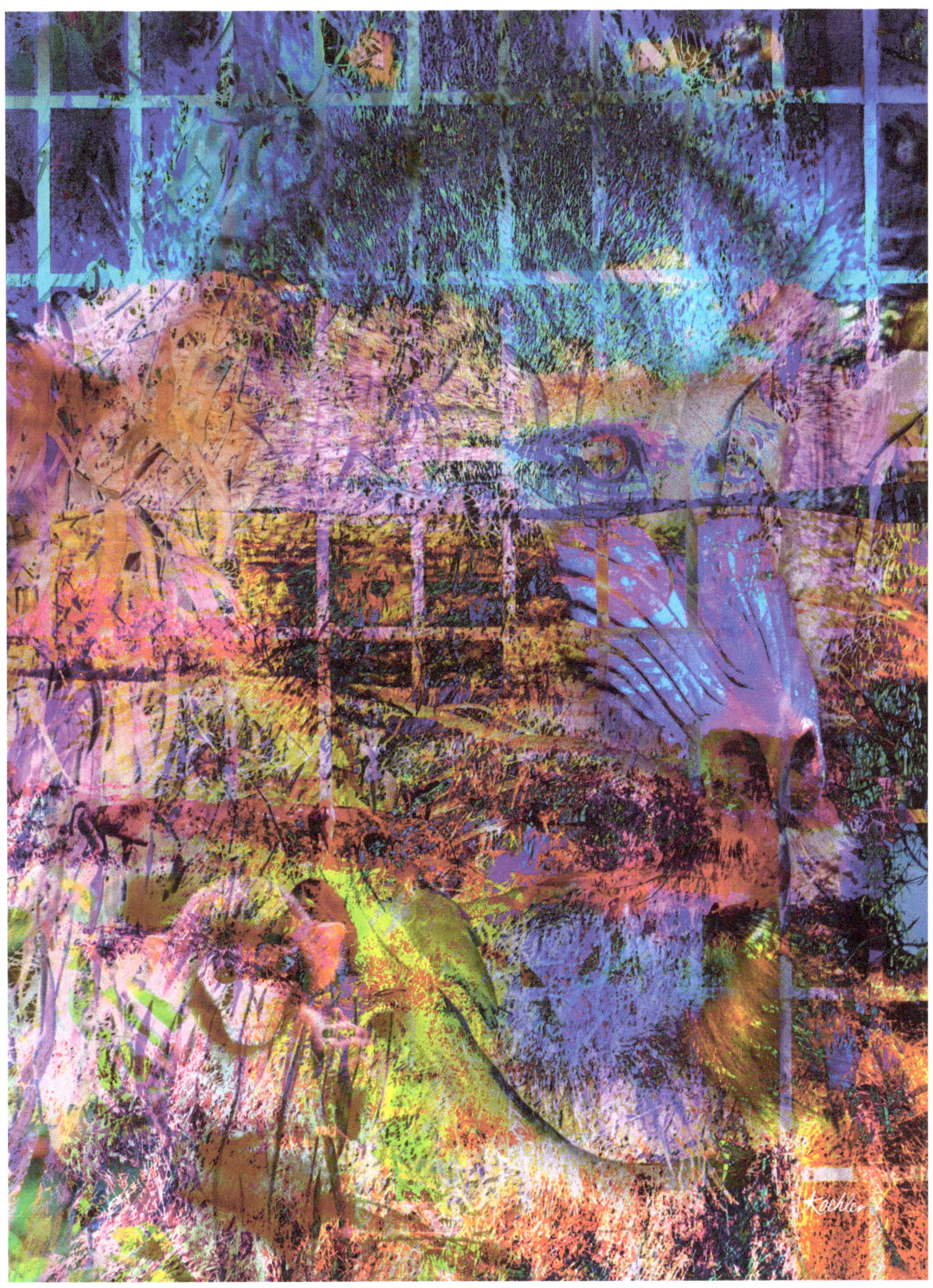

Mandrill | 2022

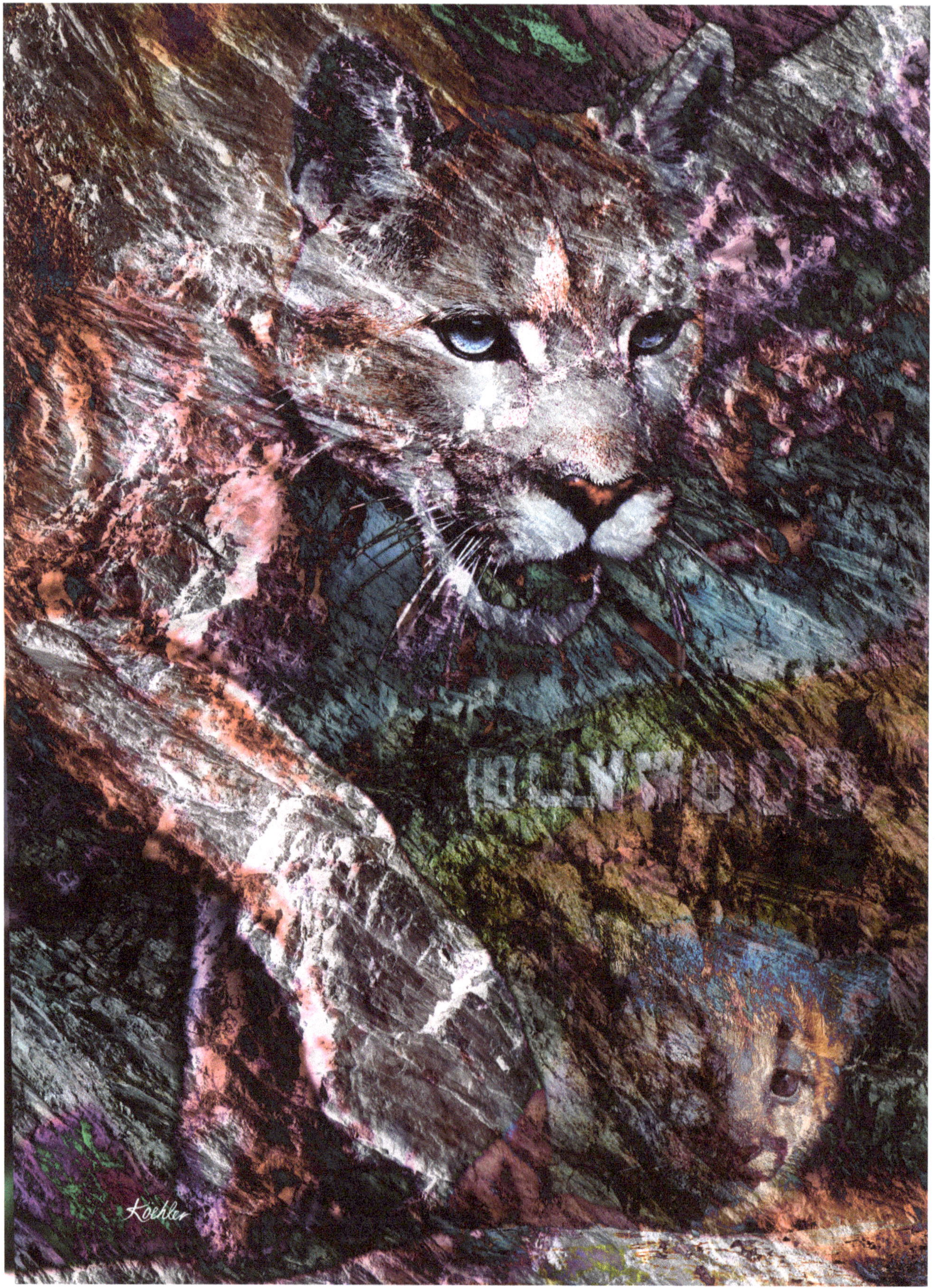

Puma | 2022

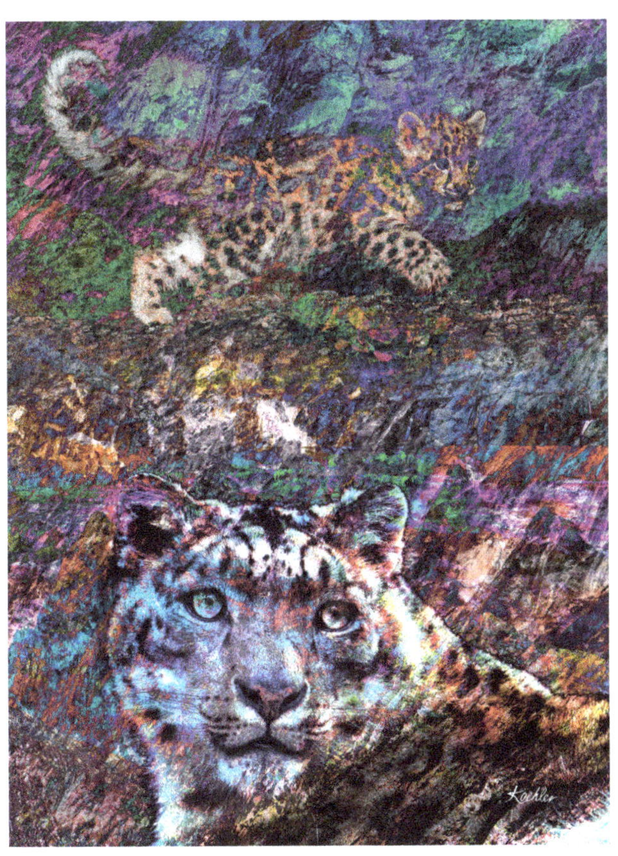

Snow Leopard | 2022

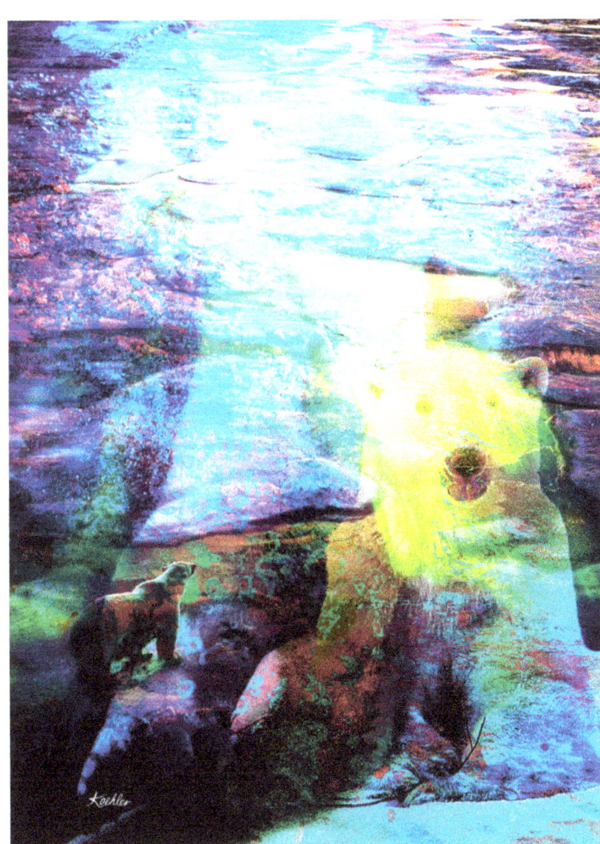

Polar Bear | 2022

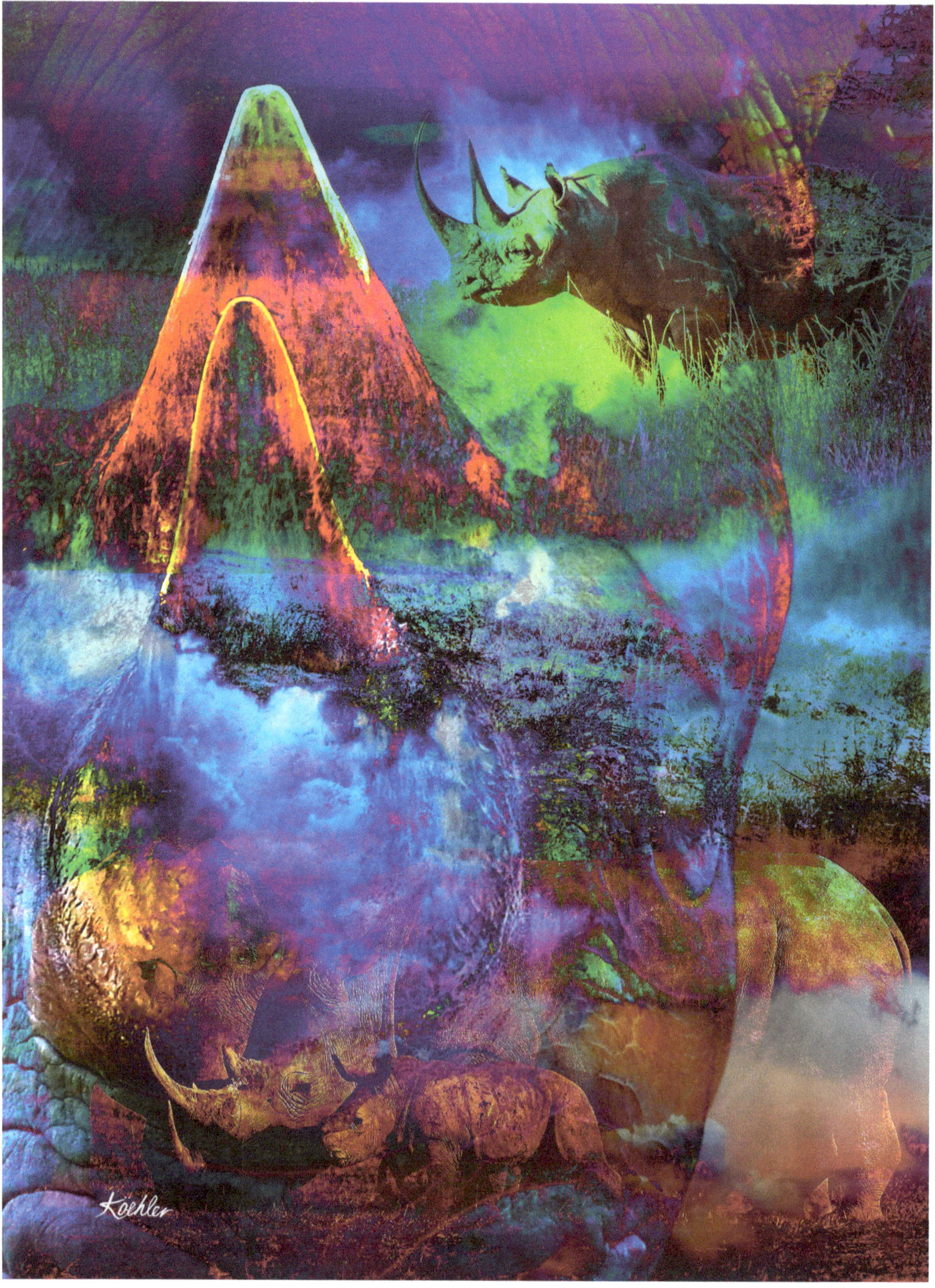

Rhino | 2022

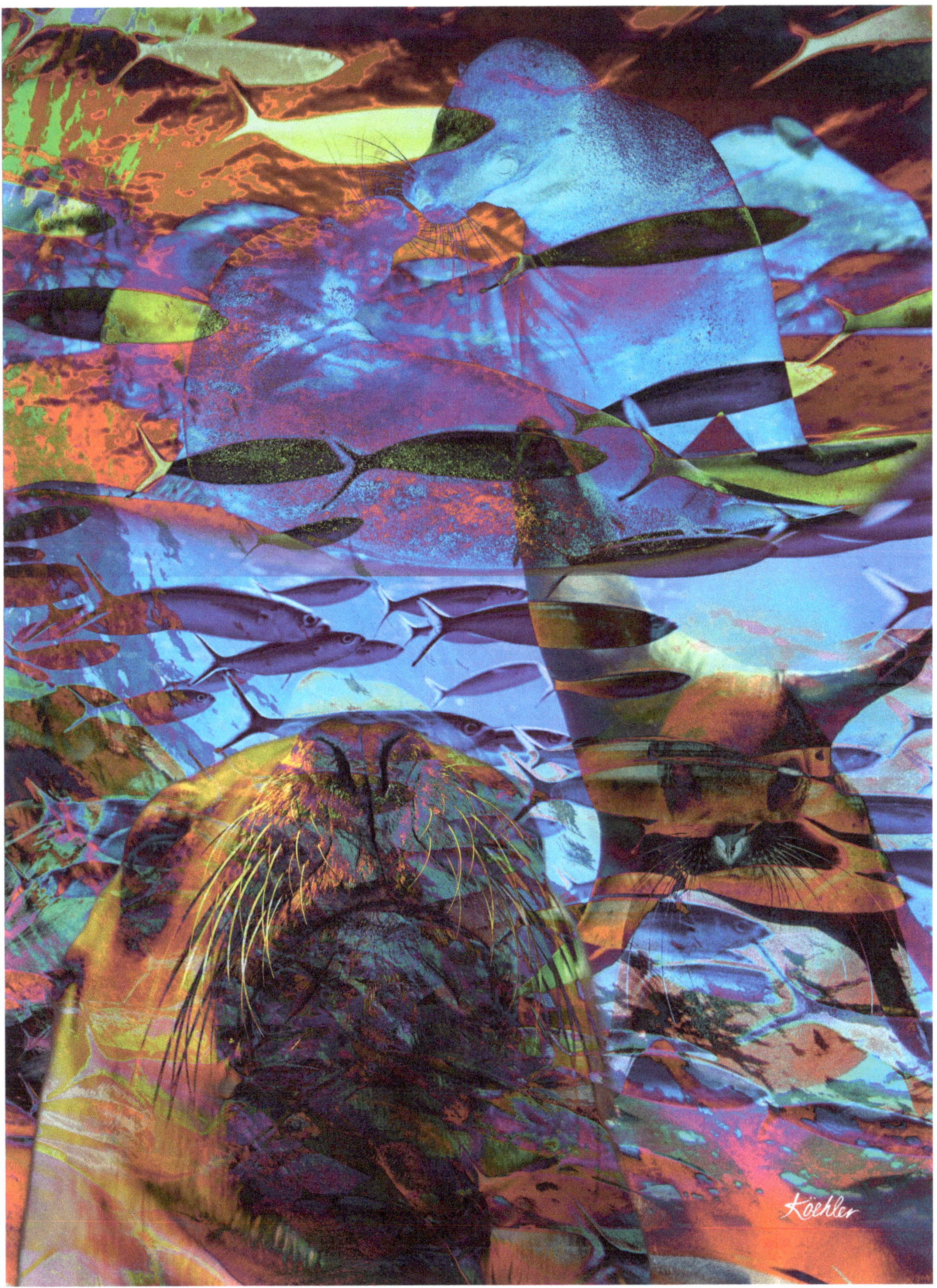

Seals | 2022

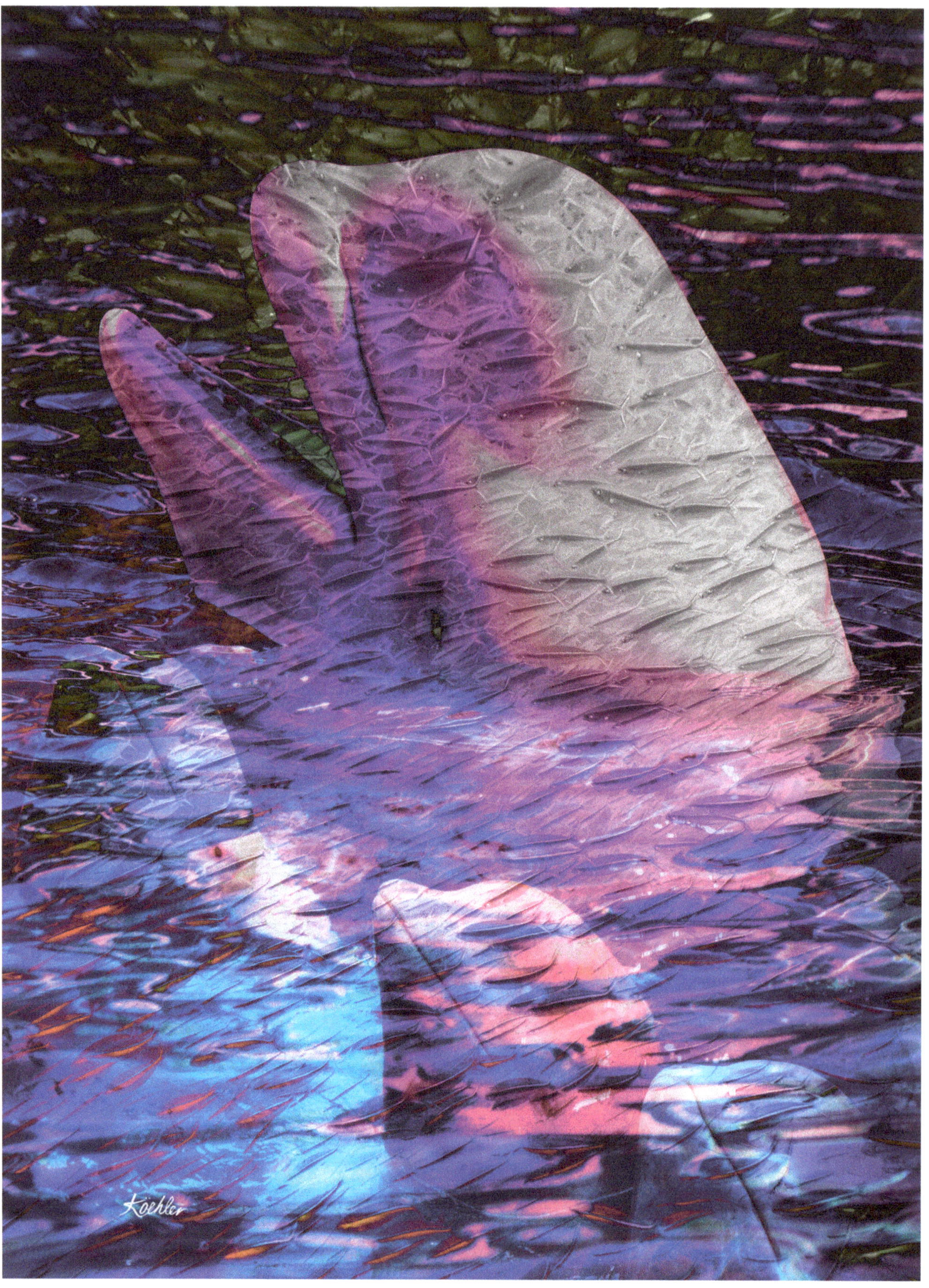

Beluga Whale | 2022

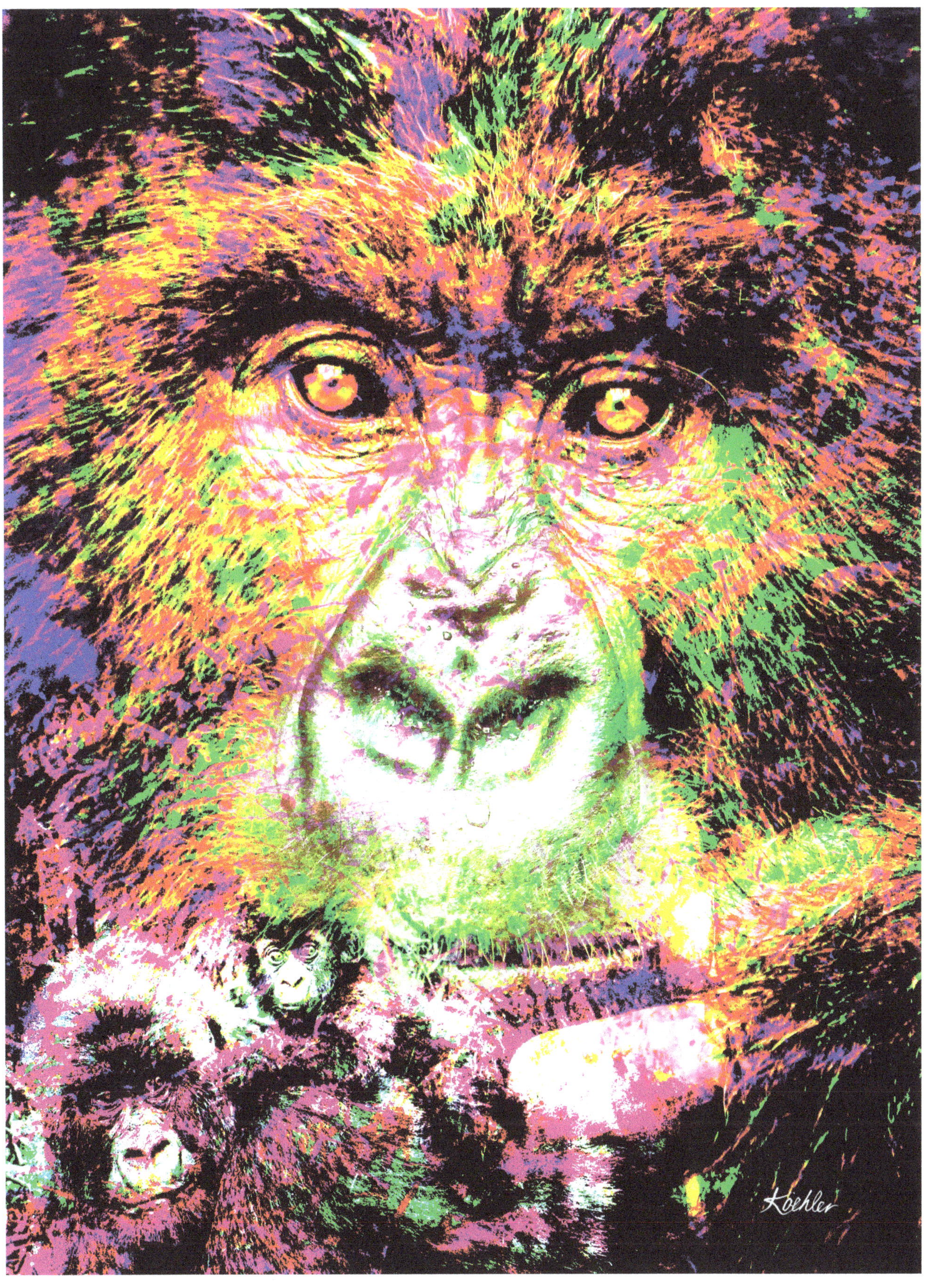

Mountain Gorilla | 2022

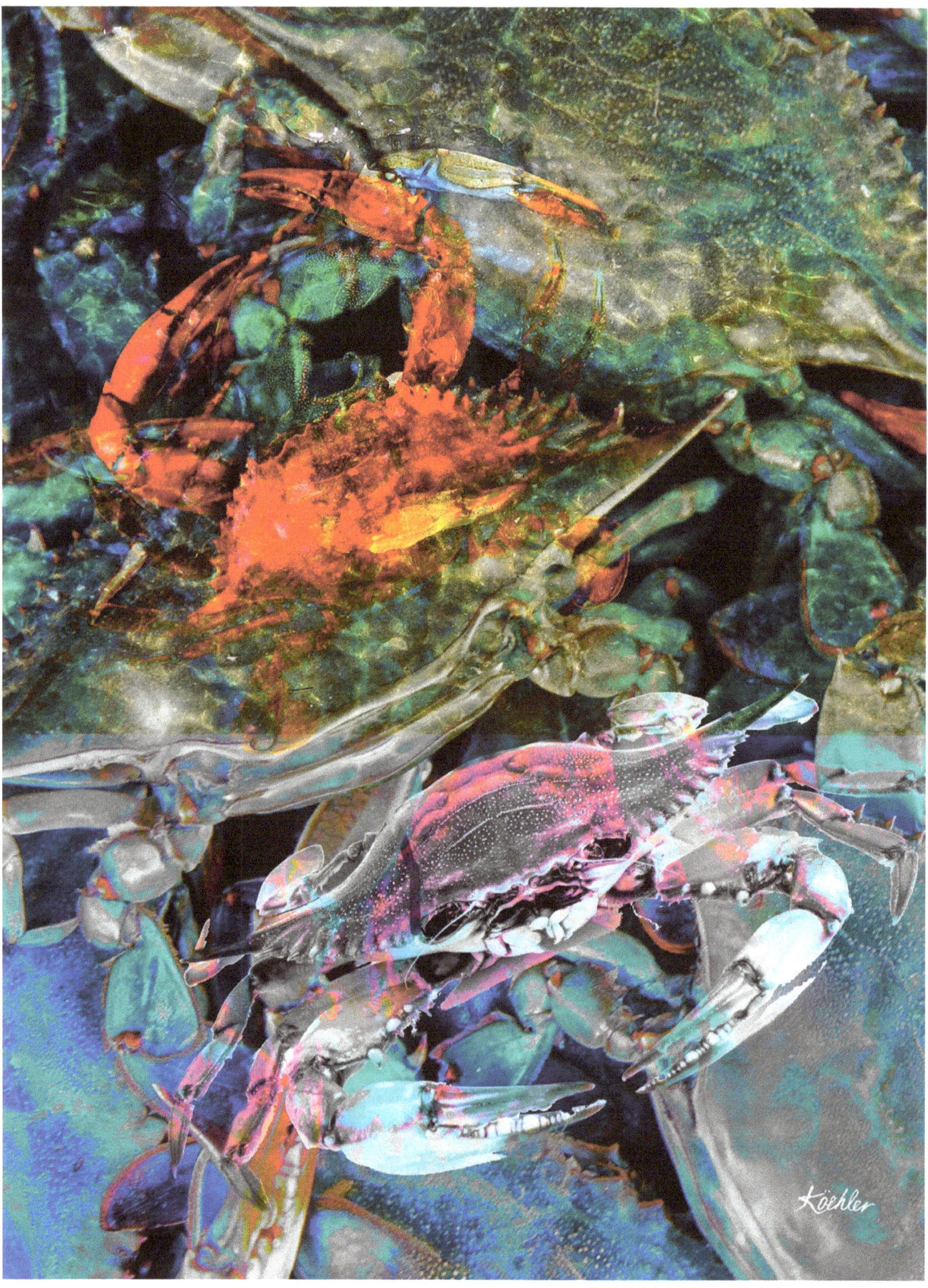

Blue Crab | 2022

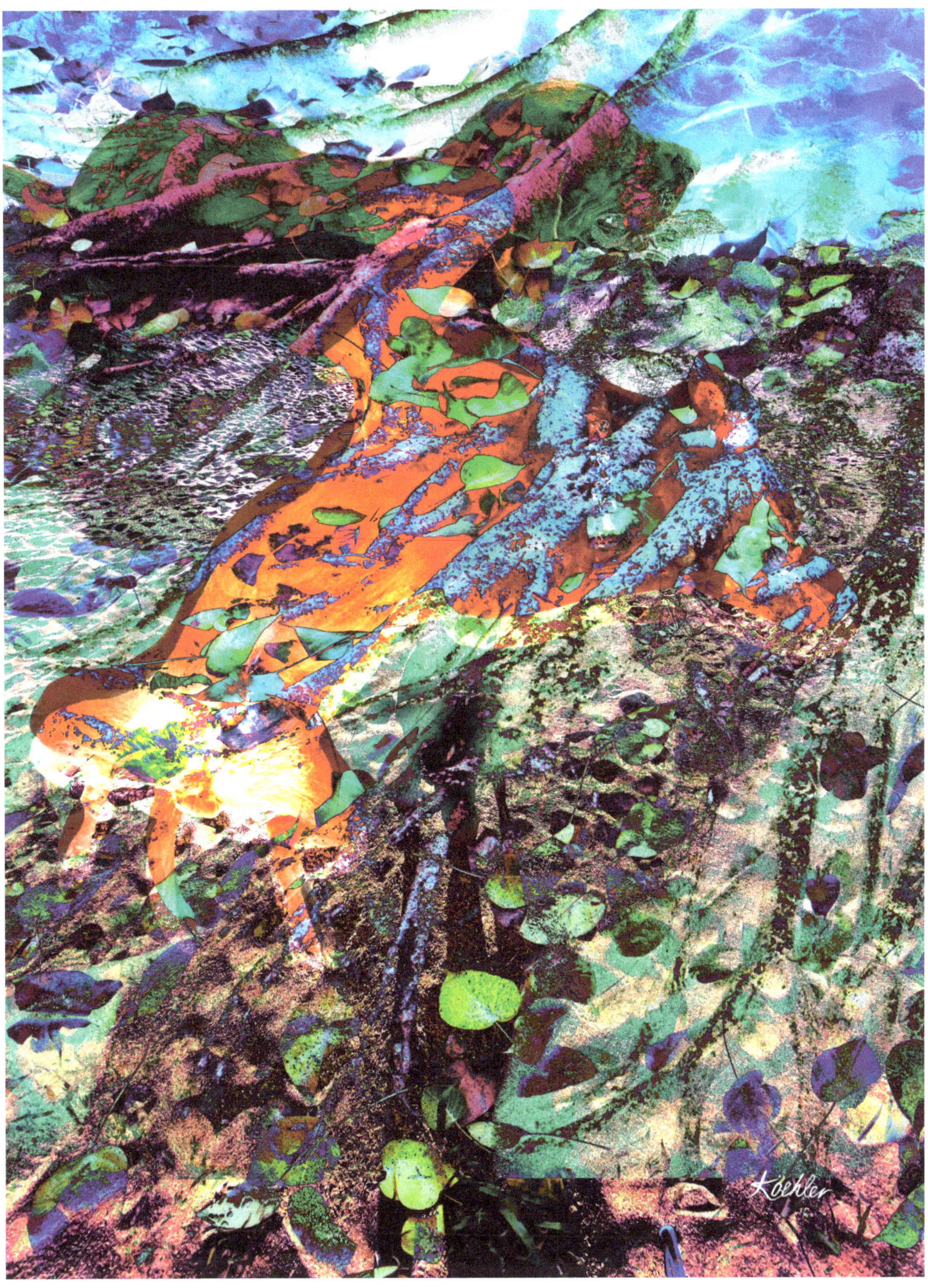

Dog Gone | 2022

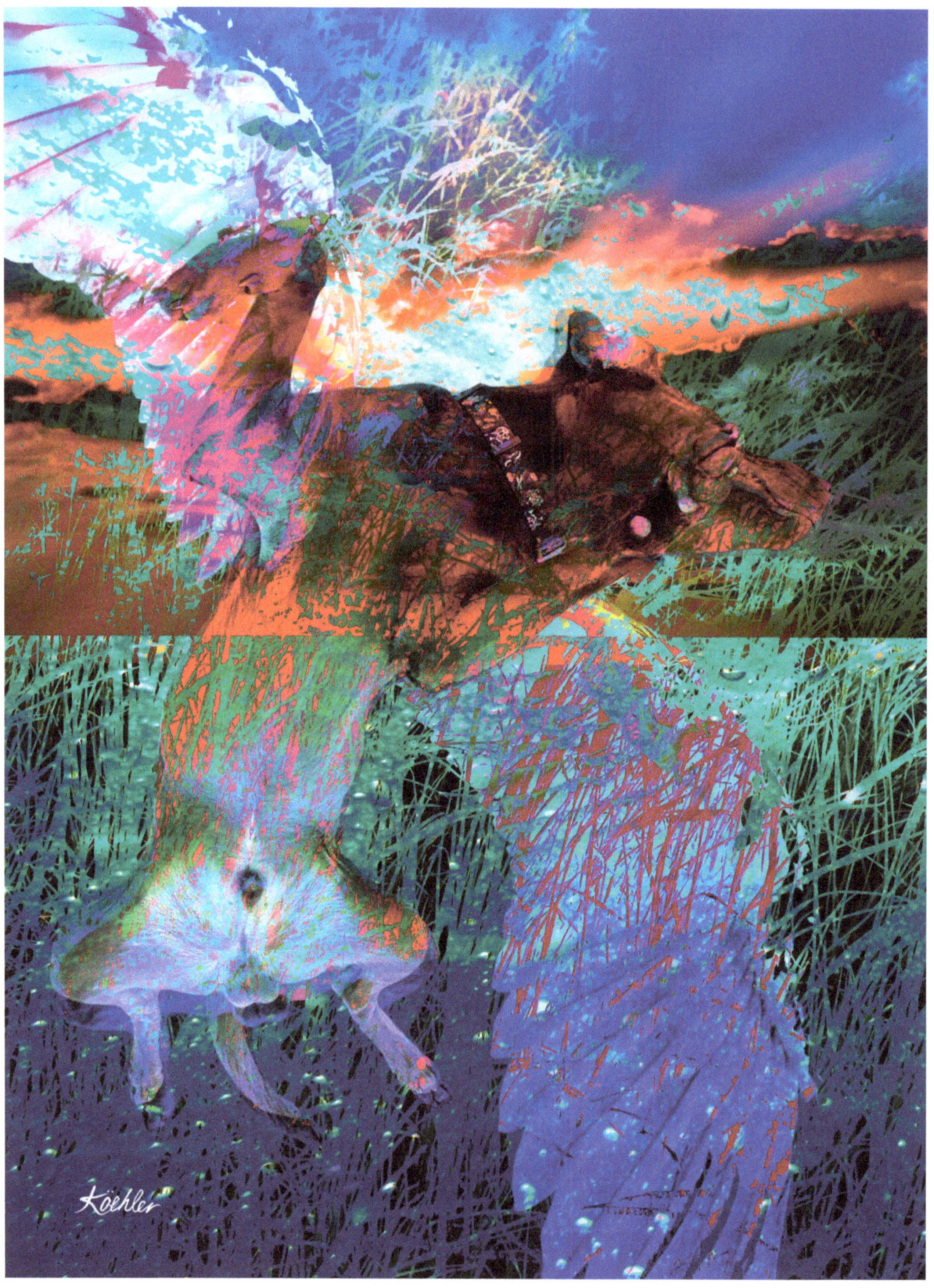

Angel Dog | 2022

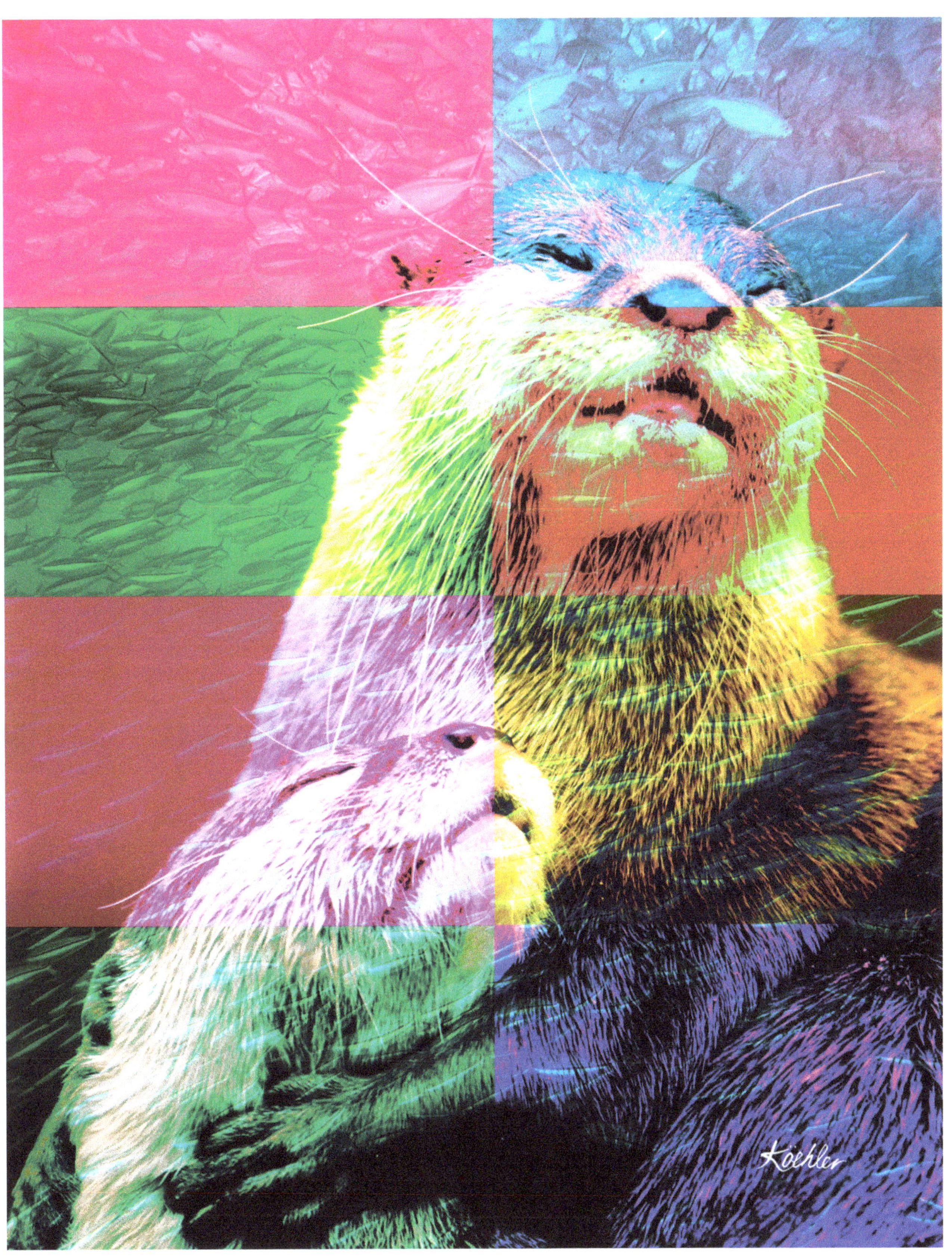

Otter Love | 2022

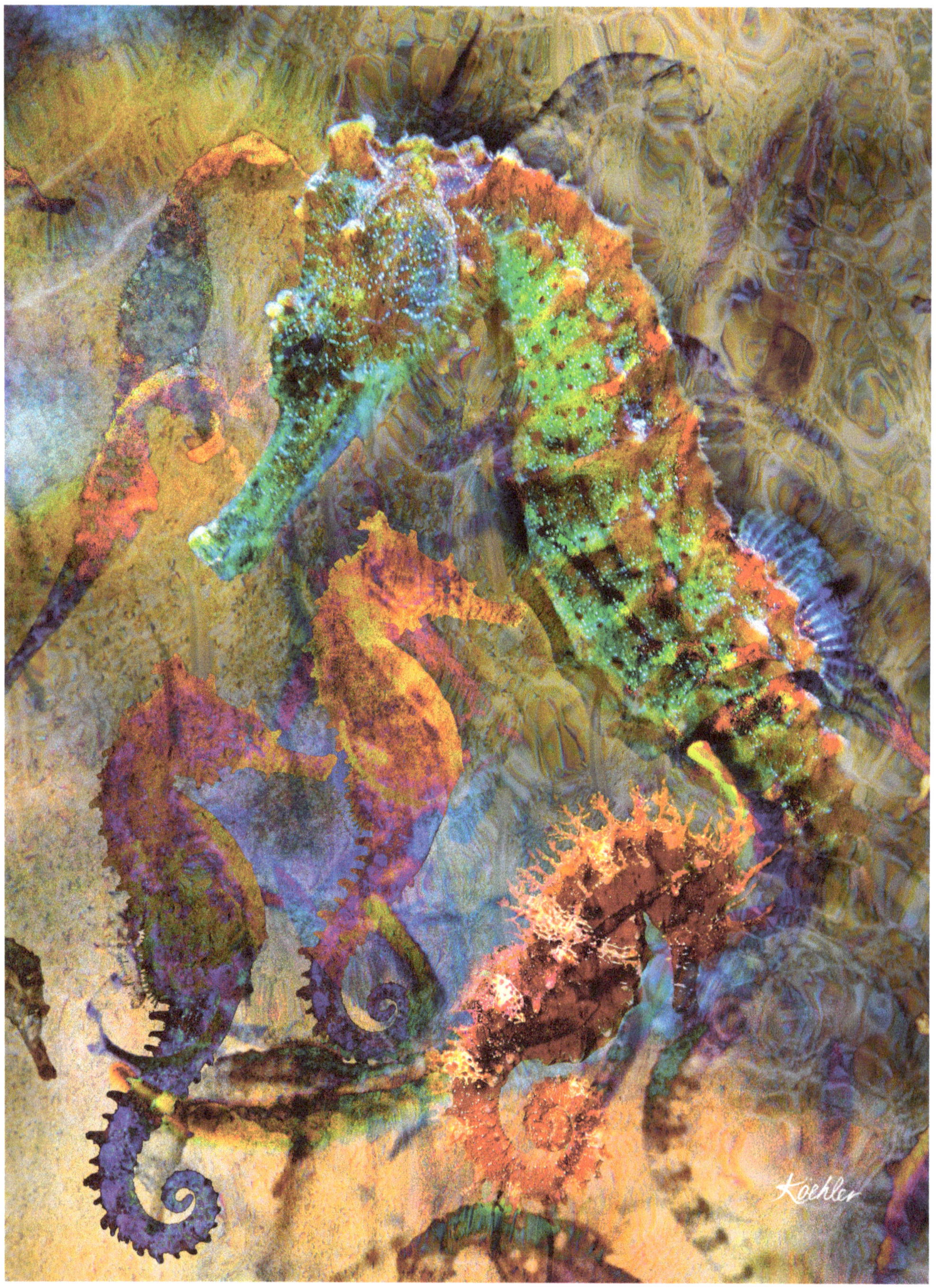

Seahorses | 2022

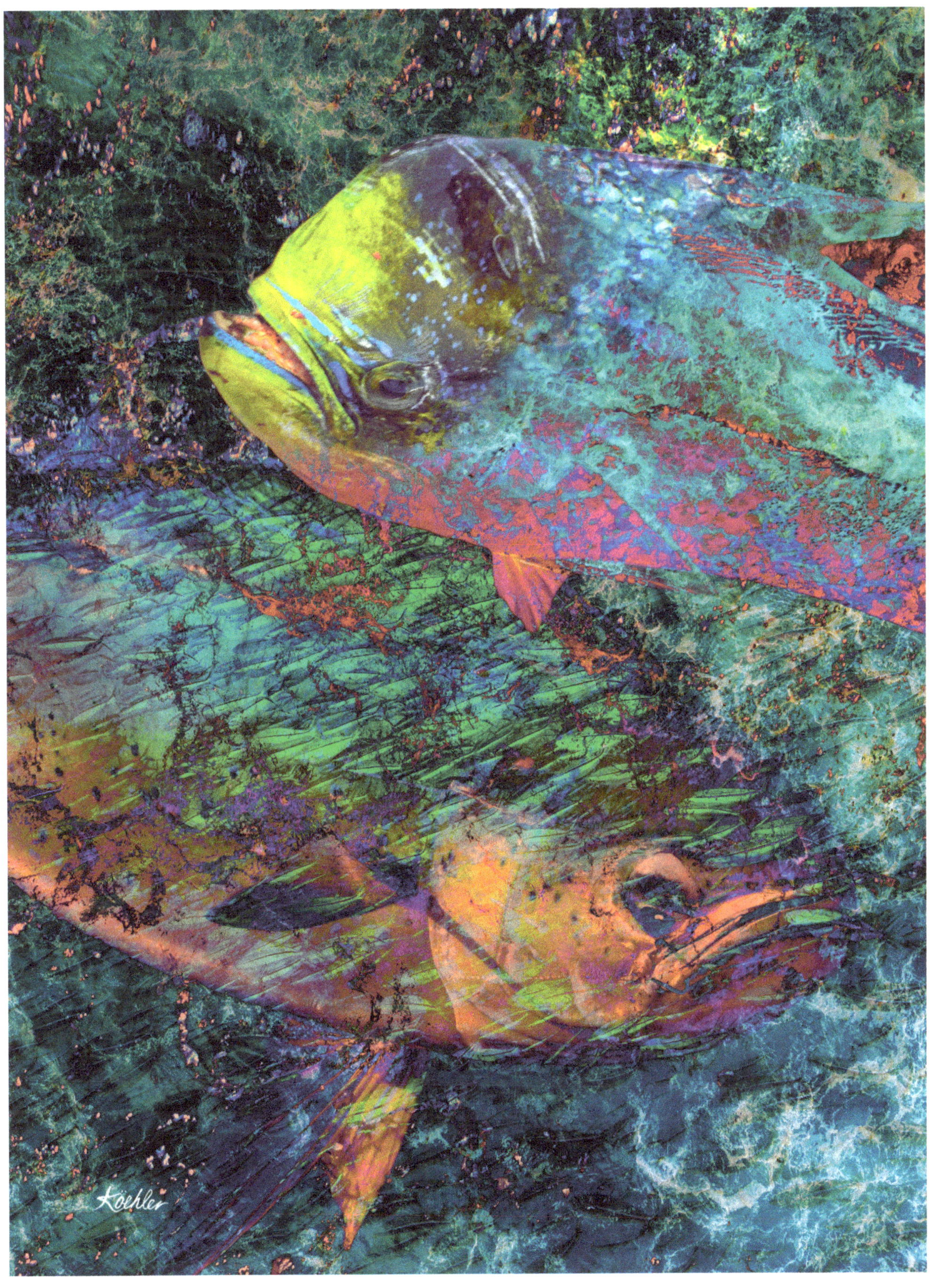

Mahi Mahi | 2022